Henry James's American Girl

The figure of the American girl is one that surfaces regularly in Henry James's fiction. Most prominent in the international novels, where the compelling portrait of an Isabel Archer or a Maggie Verver commands attention, James's girl is a complex character eager for experience yet crippled by fear, hungry for selfhood yet tragically incapable of achieving it. In this lucid exploration of James's young women, Professor Fowler examines the psychology, literary function, and cultural roots of the American girl. The result is a new perspective on James's fiction—and a reassessment of his views on feminine identity, sexual relations, and American culture—that will be of interest and value to all students of American literature, women's studies, and Henry James.

Henry James's American Girl
The Embroidery on the Canvas

Virginia C. Fowler

The University of Wisconsin Press

Published 1984

The University of Wisconsin Press
114 North Murray Street
Madison, Wisconsin 53715

The University of Wisconsin Press, Ltd.
1 Gower Street
London WC1E 6HA, England

First printing

Printed in the United States of America

ISBN 0-229-09570-3

Library of Congress Cataloging in Publication Data

Fowler, Virginia C., 1948–
  Henry James's American girl.

  Bibliography: p.
  Includes index.
  1. James, Henry, 1843–1916 — Characters — Women.
  2. James, Henry, 1843–1916 — Knowledge — United States.
  3. Women in literature. 4. United States in literature.
  I. Title.
  PS2127.W6F69 1984   813'.4   83-51050
  ISBN 0-299-09570-3

For my Mother
and
D. S.

Contents

Acknowledgments

My initial and most unrepayable debts of gratitude are to Alexander Welsh, whose graduate seminar engendered my fascination with Henry James, and to Thomas L. Philbrick, whose patient tutelage helped make possible my first extensive exploration of James's fiction.

Sincerest thanks also go to those friends and colleagues whose criticism, advice, and support through the many stages of the present project were often invaluable: Martha Banta, Arthur M. Eastman, Charles E. Modlin, Evelyn S. Newlyn, Alison G. Sulloway, and the anonymous reviewers for the Press. Many strengths of the study are attributable to their helpful comments; the weaknesses, however, remain my own.

For their most generous and valuable assistance in the mechanics of preparing the manuscript, I wish to thank Margaret Schickel and James W. Spisak.

A somewhat different version of the chapter on *The Wings of the Dove* appeared earlier in *Novel: A Forum on Fiction*; most grateful acknowledgment is made to the editors for their permission to use that material here.

Henry James's American Girl

1

The Civilizing Female:
The Symbolic Values
of the American Girl

What it came to, evidently, was that she [the American woman] had been grown in an air in which a hundred of the "European" complications and dangers didn't exist, and in which also she had had to take upon herself a certain training for freedom. It was not that she had had, in the vulgar sense, to "look out" for herself, inasmuch as it was of the very essence of her position not to be threatened or waylaid; but that she could develop her audacity on the basis of her security, just as she could develop her "powers" in a medium from which criticism was consistently absent. Thus she arrived, full-blown, on the general scene, the least criticized object, in proportion to her importance, that had ever adorned it. It would take long to say why her situation, under this retrospect, may affect the inner fibre of the critic himself as one of the most touching on record; he may merely note his perception that she was to have been after all but the sport of fate.

—The American Scene

I

When Henry James visited America in 1904, after a twenty-year absence from the land of his birth, his imagination responded not simply to the plight of America but also to that of the American woman, a figure whom he had used repeatedly in much of his early fiction and recently celebrated anew in *The Wings of the Dove* and *The Golden Bowl.* The "American girl" had been, in fact, the focal point of most of his international fiction, and even when he came to write "a very *American* tale," *The Bostonians,* he noted his conviction that "the situation of women" represented "the most salient and peculiar point in our social life."[1]

The appeal of woman to the novelist is not, of course, new with James; as Patricia Stubbs has noted, "the separation between domestic life and production, and the consequent identification of men with the external world of work and women with the internal world of feeling" led to an "ever-widening division between the private and the public" which had important consequences for the novel, not least of which was its preoccupation, especially in the nineteenth century, with heroines rather than heroes, with "love and personal relationships."[2] Still, though James can be seen as simply continuing a well-established novelistic tradition in his depiction of a private, often predominantly female world,[3] he has more often been regarded as somehow uniquely concerned with that world, as recent studies of his female characters by Mary Doyle Springer and Edward Wagenknecht attest.[4] James's contemporaries found his fiction not just concerned with females, but distinctively "feminine," a quality which they did not always explain but to which they inevitably responded. James's good friend and editor, William Dean Howells, suggested that James's male readers were "of a more feminine fineness, probably, in their perceptions and

4

intuitions, than those other men who do not read him."[5] Another contemporary, J. P. Mowbray, responded somewhat more negatively to the "femininity" of James's work; he complained that "in trying to form anything like a comprehensive estimate of Mr. James's mature work, the effeminacy of it has to be counted with. One cannot call it virile, and . . . hardly Saxon."[6] Whether this lack of "virility" in James's fiction evoked praise or, as was more frequently the case, censure, by the time F. W. Dupee came to label James, in the now classic phrase, "the great feminine novelist of a feminine age of letters,"[7] this estimate had become commonplace.

What this commonplace estimate means has not always been made clear, however, just as its denunciatory tenor has rarely been explained. Similarly, the relation of James's "exceptional identification with the feminine mind"[8] to his American identity as well as to his treatment of the American girl has been only sketchily suggested. Philip Rahv proposed that "James's so-called feminine orientation" and his predilection for the American girl, "his principal heroine," are connected by virtue of the historical fact that the American female was rising in the nineteenth century "to a position of cultural prestige and authority."[9] Rahv failed to note, however, that the new "cultural prestige and authority" being gained by the American female were matched, if not overshadowed, by the spiraling growth of industry and business, directed and controlled by the American male—a growth that seemed to James of chilling significance. Social historians like Theodore Roszak have in fact argued not only that the business and politics of the nineteenth century were controlled by men but that the "political style" of the late nineteenth century is characterized by a "compulsive masculinity."[10] This "compulsive masculinity" explains, according to Lisa Appignanesi, why James and other artists of the late nineteenth century identified art and the artist with the feminine and focused their art itself on women: "since it is men who run the world of politics, business and the mundane extensions of technology which appear to have exhausted mystery, then it is in woman that the possibilities of another order, a new resolution, a new way of viewing reality must reside. Thus the artist turns to the feminine, the mystery she still represents, and uses it as a meditational core for his art."[11]

For Henry James, of course, America embodied and symbolized this modern, "masculine" age of business and technology which, as demonstrated throughout his fiction and nonfiction, seemed to him to threaten the values of culture and civilization. America struck him, moreover, as anomalous in its absolute polarization of men and women, a polarization which resulted in an overriding masculinization of the worlds of commerce and industry and a thorough feminization of the social world. This state of affairs in America had been created, James observed, not simply because women were not admitted into the worlds of business and industry but also because "the men were consistently, in all cases, thoroughly obvious products of the 'business-block,' the business-block unmitigated by any other influence," and thus, in consequence, the women alone were left to discover "what civilization really *is*."[12]

James's complete identification of civilization with women is nowhere more strikingly apparent than in *The American Scene*, where he at one point describes America as "a society of women 'located' in a world of men, which is so different a matter from a collection of men of the world; the men supplying, as it were, all the canvas, and the women all the embroidery" *(AS*, p. 66). Through this unusual metaphor, drawn entirely from an art that is traditionally and almost without exception practiced by women, James manages to suggest that American men have really very little to do with civilization and that it is instead the province of women alone. Interesting in this connection is the fact that James often uses the same metaphor to describe his own artistic activities; in the Preface to *Roderick Hudson*, for example, he describes himself thus: "A young embroiderer of the canvas of life soon began to work in terror, fairly, of the vast expanse of that surface, of the boundless number of its distinct perforations for the needle, and of the tendency inherent in his many-coloured flowers and figures to cover and consume as many as possible of the little holes."[13] This last quotation suggests an important distinction between James the artist and the American woman, namely, that he sees himself as the *embroiderer* but sees the American woman as the *embroidery*. This distinction will become crucial in my study of the American girl. The quotations I have cited do nevertheless point to several important equivalences: James identifies his novelistic art as a feminine art; he identifies American society with the same feminine art; and he identifies women as the actual and sole representatives of civilization in America. Although the causal connections among these equations are perhaps impossible definitively to establish, the equations themselves would seem to be crucial to an understanding of James's ideas of art and society.

They also perhaps help explain his psychological characterization of his favorite female character, the American girl, the heroine whom Howells credited James with inventing[14] and who, as Rahv notes, "makes the most of his vision and dominates his drama of transatlantic relations."[15] Previous studies of James's treatment of the American girl have shown us the literary and intellectual roots of the figure. William Wasserstrom, for example, in his analysis of the genteel tradition in American fiction, has demonstrated that central to this tradition, which James both used and transformed, was the belief that "American women best represented the vigor and intensity of the American spirit."[16] And Paul John Eakin, studying the intellectual background of the nineteenth-century New England heroine, has shown that for James and for nineteenth-century society as a whole, "woman functioned as an all-purpose symbol of the ideals of the culture, the official repository of its acknowledged code."[17] No study has, however, given adequate attention to the psychology underlying James's various American girls, figures who certainly are individualized but who share common psychological conflicts created in part by a common cultural inheritance. Though James's American heroine becomes "the heiress of all the ages," she also remains in James's imagination "but the sport of fate," and this to no small degree because she alone represents "the ideals of the culture." When James suggested in *The American Scene* that

"there is such a thing, in the United States . . . as the freedom
to grow up to be blighted, and it may be the only freedom in
store for the smaller fry of future generations" (AS, p. 137), he
might well have been describing not the slum urchins of New
York but his own fictional heroines. [Inherent in James's
perception of the American heroine is the central paradox that
though in her innocence, spontaneity, and purity she offers an
alternative to the old corruption of Europe and the rampant
materialism of America, yet because she has "been grown in an
air in which a hundred of the 'European' complications and
dangers didn't exist," she often proves, as James expresses it in
The Wings of the Dove, unable to take "the whole assault of
life." She thus symbolizes for James, as Nina Auerbach has
observed, "simply and ambiguously, America itself."[18] James's
fascination with this figure resulted in some of his most
probing psychological studies, some of his most intriguing
heroines—Isabel Archer, Milly Theale, Maggie Verver—and at
the same time in some of his acutest analyses of American
culture.

This study intends to show the relation of the American
girl's psychology to the culture which nurtured it, and to
demonstrate the nature of the "blight" that afflicts both the
girl and America itself in James's international fiction. My
purpose here necessitates what is undeniably a narrow focus
on novels that are rich and complex. As is inevitable when one
employs a particular perspective, certain important aspects of
James's texts have had to suffer unavoidable neglect. But
although my interest and my emphasis in this study lie in the
psychological dimensions of a particular kind of character in
James's fiction, I do not wish to suggest that other dimensions
of his work are not equally important. Yet while the virtually
exclusive focus on the psychology of the American girl is mine
and not James's, a strong psychological strand is certainly
present and important in his depiction of this figure. An
elucidation of this strand and not a denial of others is the
primary goal of this study.

II

James's reliance on the American girl to represent the "American branch" of his "international department" *(AN,* p. 192) was necessitated, he says in the Preface to *The Reverberator,* by his own personal "incompetence" at grasping the American man: "The men . . . the fathers, brothers, playmates, male appendages of whatever presumption, were visible and thinkable only as the American 'business-man'; and before the American business-man, as I have been prompt to declare, I was absolutely and irredeemably helpless, with no fibre of my intelligence responding to his mystery" *(AN,* p. 193). Raised by Henry James, Senior, "just to be something, something unconnected with specific doing,"[19] James found himself wholly incapable of comprehending "the very alphabet of their [the businessmen's] activity" *(AN,* p. 193). Nor, he says, could he use the older, mature American woman, "the wife and mother," because "there was really, as a rule, nothing whatever to be done with the elder woman" *(AN,* p. 193). The older woman was not, like the American man, inaccessible to James by virtue of his own inability to grasp her essence; rather, her permanently fixed "blankness of surface" excluded her from consideration. James's remarks on the older American woman repay at least brief attention for the illumination they shed on the psychology and possible destiny of the American girl: "if one could work it out for the men that the depreciated state with which *they* vaguely and, as it were, somnolently struggled, was perhaps but casual and temporary, might be regarded in fact as the mere state of the medal with its right face accidentally turned down, this redemption never glimmered for the wife and mother, in whom nothing was in eclipse, but everything rather (everything there was at all) straight in evidence, and to whom therefore any round and complete embodiment had simply been denied" *(AN,* p. 193). One possibility for the American girl, presumably, would be her transformation into such a forlorn creature as her mother; James's remarks here attest, perhaps unintentionally, to the disabling potential of the American girl's psychology. But having eliminated both the American man and the American "wife and mother," James found himself "simply shut up to what was left" him—the young American girl (*AN*, p. 193).

If James's own background and experience functioned to eliminate the American man, because he was "visible and thinkable only as the American 'business-man,'" his ambivalent conception and treatment of the figure of the American girl also seem to have important autobiographical roots. At least two of James's American girls, Isabel Archer and Milly Theale, are generally acknowledged to have been based on his beloved cousin, Minny Temple; but the essential spirit of all his American girls may perhaps be traced to the haunting of his imagination by Minny, who died of tuberculosis at the age of twenty-four, when James's own artistic career was just beginning. Although Minny Temple's importance to and effect on James's life and work have been noted by his biographers and critics, the striking ambiguity inherent in his perceptions of her and in the meanings she embodied for his imagination has been ignored. On the one hand, James saw Minny, "a plant of pure American growth,"[20] as a person of tremendous life force; as he says in *Notes of a Son and Brother,* "death, at the last, was dreadful to her; she would have given anything to live," for she was "the supreme case of a taste for life as life, as personal living."[21] On the other hand, however, James viewed Minny as a person somehow unequipped for life. For example, in a letter to his mother, written on March 26, 1870, only a few weeks after Minny's death, James said that no one would have "wished her to live longer" unless he had "some irresistible mission to reconcile her to a world to which she was essentially hostile."[22] He later pursued this idea in a letter to Grace Norton: "She was a divinely restless spirit—essentially one of the 'irreconcilables'; and if she had lived to a great age, I think it would have been as the victim and plaything of her constant generous dreams and dissatisfactions."[23]

James's remarks about Minny Temple clearly point to an essential ambiguity inherent in the meanings she, the prototype of his fictional American girls, represented for him. Minny's capacity to have "at once such noble flights and such touchingly discouraged drops,"[24] which created in James "a singular mixture of pleasure and pain,"[25] is also a salient feature of James's three principal American girls, Isabel Archer, Milly Theale, and Maggie Verver. The drama in which each of these heroines figures is the encounter with Europe, the land of experience; in each of the international novels in which these heroines appear, James puts his American girl to the test of responding to "the whole assault of life." As we will see, all three of these heroines are crippled in some way; all are initially, like Minny Temple, unequipped for withstanding the assault of life, though they suffer that assault differently: Isabel Archer endures it, Milly Theale dies from it, Maggie Verver triumphs over it.

III

James's fictional heroines are, like Minny Temple, "plants of pure American growth," and James's presentation of their psychology underscores the important ways in which it results from their American roots. For this reason, before turning to an analysis of the fiction itself, we would do well to consider James's most extensive commentary on his native land, *The American Scene*. A detailed record of James's observations of American life—observations both immediate, as culled from his American tour of 1904-5, and telescopic, as reflective of perceptions gathered throughout his life—*The American Scene* furnishes us some of the particular conceptions about America and the American woman that underlie James's fictional treatments of the American girl.

As James reiterates throughout *The American Scene*, one of the central facts of American life is the complete polarization of the sexes, a condition created by the American man's abandonment of the American woman. Other visitors to America, including James's friend Paul Bourget,[26] had certainly noted this unusual situation, but for James it assumes crucial significance with regard to its effect not only on the American woman but also on the country itself. For the American man has abandoned both the woman and civilization for business;[27] thus, as we have already noted, the recurring conflict between materialism and civilization has in America become also a conflict between man and woman. Consequently, as Martha Banta suggestively observes, "whenever civilization is misused or diverted or ignored in America, the same fate is being inflicted upon the woman; and vice versa. Both nation and woman are being betrayed, and something of great value is lost."[28]

No ordinary travel book, *The American Scene* employs many poetic and novelistic devices to develop the ramifications of this enormous chasm between the American man and the American woman, between materialism and civilization. James, "the restless analyst" determined to discover the meaning of the cultural signs before him, does not give us a simple or straightforward account of the sites he visited in his tour of America. As he says, "for the restless analyst, there is no such thing as an unrelated fact, no such thing as a break in the chain of relations" *(AS,* p. 312). Thus, although the general structure of *The American Scene* approximates James's actual tour,[29] that structure has also been put to the service of explaining and elaborating upon James's principal conclusions about American life. As James remarks in the Preface to the book, "artistically concerned as I had been all my days with the human subject, with the appreciation of life itself, and with the consequent question of literary representation, I should not find such matters [as the meaning of American manners] scant or simple" *(AS,* p. ii). Consequently, we must approach *The American Scene* rather as we would approach one of James's novels.

The American Scene opens with a glimpse of New York City and a brief sketch of the New Jersey coastline, sites the book will return to in much greater detail later on. But this opening vignette functions as an appropriate introduction to the book, for it emphasizes the overriding quality which New York and, indeed, the East at large have for James, namely, the impression they give of enormous wealth being spent with little sense of purpose. At the same time, this opening sketch of the expensive houses along the New Jersey coast re-creates in the reader the anticipation experienced by James when he, newly arrived in the country after twenty years in Europe, first saw them. For the New Jersey houses seem to James to speak of a drama unfolding in America, a drama whose subject is "the great adventure of a society reaching out into the apparent void for the amenities, the consummations, after having earnestly gathered in so many of the preparations and necessities" (AS, p. 12).

If America is the stage for this particular drama, *The American Scene* itself might be viewed as staging this drama for the reader, for James, "the restless analyst," has discovered already what the closing act will be. The shape of the drama as a whole informs individual episodes as well, and it is a shape familiar to students of American literature. It might best be described as hope or promise disappointed; though indeed, by the end of *The American Scene* it is hope not simply disappointed but destroyed, annihilated.

This shape of the drama is adumbrated in the first principal episode in the book, the visit to New England. Arriving early in the autumn, James looks forward to the beauty of the landscape and anticipates an interest to be discovered in the countryside which would be "'interest' of the sort that could come easily, and therefore not of the sort—quite the contrary—that involved a consideration of the millions spent" (AS, p. 14). Such sentences pervade *The American Scene;* and they serve not simply to remind us of the ubiquity of commercialism in America but also to suggest that commercialism has appropriated our very language. Predictably, then, although James does discover much of genuine "interest" and beauty in the New England countryside, he also discovers, like the poet Robert Frost, the effect upon the New England land of the other sort of interest. For the New England countryside has been abandoned by people in search of more economically profitable farming. James thus describes the New England land as a "feminine" being who has been neglected by the "masculine" forces of commercialism because of "the proved, the notorious fact that nothing useful, nothing profitable, nothing directly economic, *could* be done [with it] at all" (AS, p. 21). James's continuation of this poetic argument figures forth the kind of relation that should obtain between feminine and masculine, between woman and man, between the interests of civilization and the interests of business: "The touching appeal of nature . . . is not so much a 'Live upon me and thrive by me' as a 'Live *with* me, somehow, and let us make out together what we may do for each other—something that is not merely estimable in more or less greasy greenbacks. See how "sympathetic" I am,' the still voice seemed everywhere to proceed, 'and how I am therefore better than my fate; see how I lend myself to poetry and sociability—positively to aesthetic use: give me that consolation'" *(AS,* p. 21).

The appeal of the feminine land has, however, gone unanswered by the masculine commercial domain, for that domain does in fact estimate everything in terms of "more or less greasy greenbacks." Moreover, the American male in his role of businessman is not only neglecting the New England land, but blighting every token of civilized life that fails to promote economic interests. This is especially evident in the way almost everything "historic," everything from the nation's past, is being swept away: "What was taking place was a perpetual repudiation of the past, so far as there had been a past to repudiate, so far as the past was a positive rather than a negative quality. There had been plenty in it, assuredly, of the negative, and that was but a shabbiness to disown or a deception to expose; yet there had been an old conscious commemorated life too, and it was this that had become the victim of supersession" *(AS,* p. 53).

The most visible "victims of supersession" in *The American Scene* are buildings, and James in fact uses America's architecture as the chief and clearest sign of her future. The reason the houses and churches and other buildings from the past are in the process of being "repudiated" is that the land on which they stand can provide sites for more economically profitable buildings; in New York City, even the universities are moveable, which leads James to ask whether that does not "quite mark the tune of the dance, of the local unwritten law that forbids almost *any* planted object to gather in a history where it stands, forbids in fact any accumulation that may not be recorded in the mere bank-book? This last became long ago *the* historic page" *(AS,* pp. 142-43). The incredible power of this economic motive in American life is made even more painfully clear to James when, after a month's absence, he revisits his old home in Boston only to find that "the act of obliteration had been breathlessly swift, and if I had often seen how fast history could be made I had doubtless never so felt that it could be unmade still faster. It was as if the bottom had fallen out of one's own biography, and one plunged backward into space without meeting anything" *(AS,* p. 229).

The symbol of this destruction of the past, of the substitution of the bank-book for the "historic page," is the skyscraper. Virtually the only kind of architecture on the American scene, it becomes for James a symbol of "that perpetual passionate pecuniary purpose which plays with all forms, which derides and devours them" *(AS,* p. 111). The skyscraper is also an obviously male symbol, and the dominant feature of New York City, to which, as his birthplace, James not unnaturally devotes a significant portion of *The American Scene.* Of the skyscrapers in New York he remarks: "Crowned not only with no history, but with no credible possibility of time for history, and consecrated by no uses save the commercial at any cost, they are simply the most piercing notes in that concert of the expensively provisional into which your supreme sense of New York resolves itself" *(AS,* p. 77).

The masculine skyscraper not only instantly destroys "quality in everything it overtowers" *(AS,* p. 232), but also is itself inherently ugly. James finds particularly ugly and significant the endless rows of windows that dominate the facades of the skyscrapers: "Doesn't it take in fact acres of window glass to help even one expert New Yorker to get the better of another expert one, or to see that the other expert one doesn't get the better of *him?* It is easy to conceive that, after all, with this origin and nature stamped upon their foreheads, the last word of the mercenary monsters should not be their address to our sense of formal beauty" *(AS,* p. 96).

If New York City itself is for James like a "'bold bad' charmer," a "bad bold beauty," a "compromised charmer" *(AS,* pp. 108-10) who is suffering the assault of the hideous skyscraper, it seems perhaps inevitable that the other perversion on the scene is the hotel; in fact, next to the skyscraper, nothing on the American scene is more ubiquitous than the hotel, from the Waldorf-Astoria in New York to The Royal Poinciana in Palm Beach, the description of which constitutes one of the final episodes of *The American Scene*. Early in the book, James asks himself whether "the hotel-spirit may not just *be* the American spirit most seeking and most finding itself" *(AS,* p. 102). Although one might initially assume that the hotel would function as a positive symbol—as traditionally in literature and in life the hospitality of the inn and the innkeeper have functioned—this does not prove to be the case; for the hotel must provide housing for those who visit the "compromised charmer." Consequently, the hotel represents to James the complete abolition of privacy and of decency: "Here was a world whose relation to its form and medium was practically imperturbable; here was a conception of publicity *as* the vital medium organized with the authority with which the American genius for organization, put on its mettle, alone could organize it" *(AS,* p. 105).

Instead, then, of extending the traditionally positive values associated with the home and retained by the small inn, the hotel in America has destroyed those values. And the extent to which the "hotel spirit" is "the American spirit most seeking and most finding itself" can be seen in the way this spirit has invaded and transformed the private home in America. Moreover, as the sexual dimension of the language used to describe the American home in the following passage makes clear, the publicity of American life created by the masculine forces of commercialism has destroyed values explicitly associated with woman:

> Thus we have the law fulfilled that every part of every house shall be, as nearly as may be, visible, visitable, penetrable, not only from every other part, but from as many parts of as many other houses as possible, if they only be near enough. Thus we see systematized the indefinite extension of all spaces and the definite merging of all functions; the enlargement of every opening, the exaggeration of every passage, the

substitution of gaping arches and far perspectives and resounding voids for enclosing walls, for practicable doors, for controllable windows, for all the rest of the essence of the room-character, that room-suggestion which is so indispensable not only to occupation and concentration, but to conversation itself, to the play of the social relation at any other pitch than the pitch of a shriek or a shout. This comprehensive canon has so succeeded in imposing itself that it strikes you as reflecting inordinately . . . the social tone that has dictated it. *(AS,* p. 167)

As the sexual overtones of the imagery in this passage attest, the masculine forces in American life, through their repeated assaults, are destroying all that is feminine and all that is civilized in that life. This idea gains more forceful expression when James continues his description; the visitor to an American home, he says, encounters something not unlike a brothel[30] because that visitor "sees only doorless apertures, vainly festooned, which decline to tell him where he is, which make him still a homeless wanderer, which show him other apertures, corridors, staircases, yawning, expanding, ascending, descending, and all as for the purpose of giving his presence 'away,' of reminding him that what he says must be said for the house" *(AS,* p. 168).

Where in American life have the feminine values, the civilized values, been left unmolested, undestroyed? At best, James suggests, one will find only occasional oases in the midst of the deserts which America's cities are becoming. Such an oasis, in New York, is Central Park, which James interestingly compares to the "cheerful, capable, bustling, even if overworked hostess of the one" and only inn in town *(AS,* p. 175). But poor Central Park must "do" far more than any one civilized oasis can do, since "it has had to have something for everybody, since everybody arrives famished" *(AS,* p. 176). Thus, despite the lengthy, lyrical tribute that James devotes to the feminine park, it is incapable of holding its own against, let alone of overshadowing, the skyscrapers and hotels.

Leaving New York, James finds similar aspects in other

places in the East. In Newport, for example, he discovers that the "process of injection and elaboration, of creating the palpable pile, had been going on for years to such a tune that the face of nature was now as much obliterated as possible, and the original shy sweetness as much as possible bedizened and bedevilled" *(AS,* p. 211). And in Boston, the Athenaeum, the museum of art, has been overshadowed by the skyscraper; its plight thus speaks most emphatically to the restless analyst:

> Put completely out of countenance by the mere masses of brute ugliness beside it, the temple of culture looked only rueful and snubbed, hopelessly down in the world. . . . the brute masses, above the comparatively small refined facade (one saw how happy one had always thought it) having for the inner ear the voice of a pair of school bullies who hustle and pummel some studious little boy. "'Exquisite' was what they called you, eh? We'll teach you, then, little sneak, to be exquisite! We allow none of that rot round here!" It was heart-breaking, this presentation of a Boston practically void of an Athenaeum. *(AS,* pp. 232-33)

Such are the dominant notes struck throughout the first half of *The American Scene,* where James describes his impressions of Vermont, New York, Boston, Philadelphia—the earliest roots of the Republic. Consistently, what he finds to be the basis of life here is the "basis . . . of active pecuniary gain and of active pecuniary gain only" *(AS,* p. 236). That basis he presents as a singlemindedly masculine one which is destroying the feminine values of civilization. While James notes that these masculine concerns are in fact pursued exclusively by the American man and that, similarly, the feminine values of civilization have been left exclusively to the American woman, he makes clear the fact that this division is as unnecessary as it is dangerous. He reflects, for example, upon the Harvard undergraduate and wonders: "In what proportion of instances would it stick out that the canvas, rather than the embroidery, was what he had to show? In what proportion would he wear the stamp of the unredeemed commercialism that should betray his paternity? In what proportion, in his appearance, would the different social 'value' imputable to his mother have succeeded in interposing?" *(AS*, p. 66). In point of fact, however, nowhere in this section of *The American Scene* do we see this schism being bridged by the American man.

IV

The first half of James's book is devoted, as we have seen, to the North and the East; the second half is devoted to the South; and between these two sections of the country and of the book as well we find interposed Washington, D. C. The North, we saw, is dominated by the masculine spirit of commercialism that is busily destroying all tokens of the nation's history, all tokens of civilized life. Clearly, the destructive energy of the North, symbolized by the towering skyscraper, represents for James the future of the nation. The South, by contrast, as we will see, represents the past, a past which James seems to suggest can serve as a warning to the North and the direction it is taking. But between the North and the South, serving symbolically as a transitional spot, is Washington. Significantly, of all the places described in *The American Scene*, Washington is the single spot that provokes an uncompromisingly positive response.

Behind James's response to Washington lie two important facts: one, its indifference to the "vulgar vociferous Market" *(AS*, p. 342), and the other, the reappearance in Washington society of the American man. In Washington and in Washington only, the American man is something other than a businessman: "Nobody was in 'business'—that was the sum and substance of it; and for the one large human assemblage on the continent of which this was true the difference made was huge. . . . The value here was at once that the place could offer to view a society, the only one in the country, in which Man existed, and that that rich little fact became the key to everything" *(AS*, p. 345). The "everything" to which James finds the key in Washington is the general polarization of the sexes throughout the rest of the country, and the implications of that polarization. For everywhere in the country, the woman "has made [life] over in her image" because the man has devoted himself exclusively to business *(AS*, p. 345); in America, then, one finds "the *successful* rupture of a universal law," the law by which men and women elsewhere labor together to create civilization.

The rupture of this law has resulted in the complete and sole domination of the social field by the woman, a state of affairs that is not in the best interest of either woman or civilization:

> Why need she originally . . . have embraced so confidently, so gleefully, yet so unguardedly, the terms offered her to an end practically so perfidious? Why need she, unless in the interest of her eventual discipline, have turned away with so light a heart after watching the Man, the deep American man, retire into his tent and let down the flap? She had her "paper" from him, their agreement signed and sealed; but would she not, in some other air and under some other sky, have been visited by a saving instinct? Would she not have said, "No, this is too unnatural; there must be a trap in it somewhere—it's addressed really, in the long run, to making a fool of me"? *(AS*, p. 348)

If the American man's abandonment of the American woman has been "addressed really, in the long run, to making a fool of" her, James nevertheless wonders how the woman in Washington will respond to the re-entry of the man on the social scene she has dominated. Yet the answer he finds there is hardly surprising: "Nowhere more than in Washington, positively, were the women to have struck me as naturally and harmoniously in the social picture—as happily, soothingly, proportionately, and no more than proportionately, participant and ministrant. Hence the irresistible conclusion that with the way really shown them they would only ask to take it; the way being their assent to the truth that the abdication of the Man proves ever (after the first flush of their triumph) as bad really for their function as for his" *(AS*, p. 351).

Although James does not elaborate on or really define what the respective "functions" of men and women in a society are or should be, it is certainly clear that the total dominance by either one is ultimately undesirable. And at this point it is perhaps worth recalling the remarks James made about Saint-Beuve, who he thought incorporated both masculine and feminine qualities:

> There is something feminine in his tact, his penetration, his subtlety and pliability, his rapidity of transition, his magical divinations, his sympathies and antipathies, his marvellous art of insinuation, of expressing himself by fine touches and of adding touch to touch. But all this side of the feminine genius was in Saint-Beuve reinforced by faculties of quite another order—faculties of the masculine stamp—the completeness, the solid sense, the constant reason, the moderation, the copious knowledge, the passion for exactitude and for general considerations. In attempting to appreciate him, it is impossible to keep these things apart.[31]

Although James tends in *The American Scene* to view civilized values as somehow feminine, this tendency would seem to be the result of that schism in American life between commercialism and civilization, between men and women. In point of fact, as his comments on Saint-Beuve make clear, civilized values are no less "masculine" than "feminine," though the absolute differences in sexual roles in America lead James—and the unwary reader—into assuming as much.

A completely feminized culture is indeed something James finds undesirable, as is evident from his description of the South. If in the North society is run by women and business by men, with no possible overlap of the two, in the South we seem to find only women, women attempting to patch together the remnants left of their culture. James depicts the South as a place of utter desolation, and he finds that desolation the natural result of the ideals the South tried to realize: "I was tasting, mystically, of the very essence of the old Southern idea—the hugest fallacy, as it hovered there to one's backward, one's ranging vision, for which hundreds of thousands of men had ever lain down their lives. I was tasting of the very bitterness of the immense, grotesque, defeated project—the project extravagant, fantastic, and to-day pathetic in its folly, of a vast Slave State (as the old term ran) artfully, savingly isolated in the world that was to contain it and trade with it" *(AS*, p. 371). Repeatedly, the condition of the South is for James the condition "of having worshipped false gods" *(AS*, p. 394). One result of the South's defeat, moreover, is its complete feminization: "The feminization is there just to promote for us some eloquent antithesis; just to make us say that whereas the ancient order was masculine, fierce and moustachioed, the present is at the most a sort of sick lioness who has so visibly parted with her teeth and claws that we may patronizingly walk all round her" *(AS*, p. 417).

Rich in its suggestiveness, this short passage perhaps contains a key to the overall structure of *The American Scene*. If the South is now completely feminized, "a sort of sick lioness," James suggests that the reason for this present condition is that in the past the South was utterly masculine, "fierce and moustachioed." The idea of a slave state is, of course, an eminently patriarchal idea, but it is also, James indicates in the earlier passage, an "extravagant" and "fantastic" idea. A masculine idea fantastical and doomed to failure has led, then, to the current sickly and completely feminized South. I would suggest that James's structure in *The American Scene* posits an analogy between this condition of the South and the causes that brought it about, and the possible future to be brought about by the North's perverse and exclusive dedication to masculine commercialism. For the movement of the book is from the North to the South; and James clearly finds the North's singleminded devotion to commercialism as absurd and fantastical and doomed a pursuit as he found the South's devotion to the idea of a slave state. His depiction of the South, then, can be seen as a sort of warning to the nation at large.

The final half of *The American Scene* does not, however, express any real hope that the lesson of the South will be heeded by America. On the contrary, the farther south James travels, the more pessimistic becomes the general tone of the book. The principal symbol of this section of *The American Scene* is the train that carries James southward. The final

destination of the train is Florida, which functions in the book
as the apotheosis of the hotel spirit, a spirit resulting from the
pursuit of economic gain and producing a shabby, sordid,
contemptible social scene that is ultimately repulsive. Reading
the final chapters of *The American Scene,* one is indeed
oppressed by the meanness and smallness and drabness that
James found enshrined in American life:

> The jealous cultivation of the common mean, the
> common mean only, the reduction of everything to an
> average of decent suitability, the gospel of precaution
> against the dangerous tendency latent in many things to
> become too good for their context, so that persons
> partaking of them may become too good for their
> company—the idealized form of all this glimmered for
> me, as an admonition or a betrayal, through the
> charming Florida radiance, constituting really the
> greatest interest of the lesson one had travelled so far to
> learn. . . . Definitely, one had made one's pilgrimage but
> to find the hotel-spirit in sole *articulate* possession. *(AS,*
> p. 442)

This meanness and mediocrity, this intellectual squalor,
James attributes to the equalizing force of democracy. A
further result of that force is a sickening falsification and
pretension, evident in the nation's arts as well as in its myth-
making:

> No long time is required, in the States, to make vivid for
> the visitor the truth that the nation is almost feverishly
> engaged in producing, with the greatest possible activity
> and expedition, an "intellectual" pabulum after its own
> heart, and that not only the arts and ingenuities of the
> draftsman (called upon to furnish the picturesque
> background and people it with the "aristocratic" figure
> where neither of these revelations ever meets his eye) pay
> their extravagant tribute, but that those of the journalist,
> the novelist, the dramatist, the genealogist, the historian,
> are pressed as well, for dear life, into the service. *(AS,* p.
> 458)

Passages such as these are frequent in the final chapters of

The American Scene and they seem to complete for the reader that downward arc of the expectation-disappointment paradigm that shapes the book's individual episodes and its overall structure. For although James clearly finds appalling the dedication to commerce which dominates the first half of *The American Scene,* there is nevertheless in those pages a sense of energy and life that is missing in the last half of the book. The dramatic movement thus seems to climax with the unexpected affirmation found in the Washington section, where for once the American man is not engaged simply in business but has in fact rejoined the American woman in the pursuit of a civilized life they both can share. But the reader is not allowed to find in Washington a lasting or final affirmation or hope. For the journey southward forces upon our minds the recognition that the rest of the country is pursuing something other than a civilized life.

It is, again, in the final sections of the book, a masculine energy misdirected that James metaphorically indicts for the destruction of civilized values. *The American Scene* concludes with James once more aboard the train, this time headed north, out of the "forward" Southern spring—a false spring—and into the "backward" Northern winter—even the seasons seem to have become unnatural. And as he crosses the land, he imagines the turning wheels saying, over and over, "see what I'm making of all this, see what I'm making of all this," to which he responds:

> "I see what you are *not* making, oh, what you are ever so vividly not; and how can I help it if I am subject to that lucidity?—which appears never so welcome to you, for its measure of truth, as it ought to be! How can I not be so subject, from the moment I don't irreflectively gape? If I were one of the painted savages you have dispossessed, or even some tough reactionary trying to emulate him, what you are making would doubtless impress me more than what you are leaving unmade; for in that case it wouldn't be to *you* I should be looking in any degree for beauty or for charm. Beauty and charm would be for me in the solitude you have ravaged, and I should owe you my grudge for every disfigurement and every violence, for

every wound with which you have caused the face of the land to bleed. No, since I accept your ravage, what strikes me is the long list of arrears of your undone; and so constantly, right and left, that your pretended message of civilization is but a colossal recipe for the *creation* of arrears, and of such as can but remain forever out of hand. You touch the great lonely land—as one feels it still to be—only to plant upon it some ugliness about which, never dreaming of the grace of apology or contrition, you then proceed to brag with a cynicism all your own. You convert the large and noble sanities that I see around me, you convert them one after the other to crudities, to invalidities, hideous and unashamed; and you so leave them to add to the number of the myriad aspects you simply spoil, of the myriad unanswerable questions that you scatter about as some monstrous unnatural mother might leave a family of unfathered infants on doorsteps or in waiting-rooms. This is the meaning surely of the inveterate rule that you shall multiply the perpetrations you call 'places'—by the sign of some name as senseless, mostly, as themselves—to the sole end of multiplying to the eye, as one approaches, every possible source of displeasure. When nobody cares or notices or suffers, by all one makes out, when no displeasure, by what one can see, is ever felt or ever registered, why shouldn't you, you may indeed ask, be as much in your right as you need? But in that fact itself, that fact of the vast general unconsciousness and indifference, looms, for any restless analyst who may come along, the accumulation, on your hands, of the unretrieved and the irretrievable!" *(AS*, pp. 463-64)

Some of the images in this powerful passage are particularly significant to the connections between women and civilization that James makes throughout *The American Scene.* To the aggressive masculine spirit of the train, James protests that it is engaged in creating greater and greater "arrears"; instead of opening up the Indians' land in order to bring civilization to it, this industrial, commercial spirit is in fact transforming the good into the bad. The "noble sanities" of nature are thus "converted" into the "crudities" and "invalidities" of "civilization." In a final twist, James compares this masculine spirit of the train to a "monstrous unnatural mother" who abandons her "unfathered infants"—a simile that both captures the perverse polarization of the sexes in America and insists that the destruction of civilized life is a perversion of what is quintessentially feminine.

V

If James thus senses that both America's natural and her civilized landscapes are being blighted or destroyed by a masculine energy horribly, perversely misdirected, he recognizes also the consequences of this fact for the young American woman, the "exposed maiden." For it is clear to him that the development of the American man into a kind of money-producing monster must inescapably and profoundly affect the American woman. He articulates his awareness of this impact, for example, when he ponders the traveling salesmen, who are wholly anomalous beings in his eyes: "what happened, inconceivably, when such Greeks met such Greeks, such faces looked into such faces, and such sounds, in especial, were exchanged with such sounds? What women did they live with, what women, living with them, could yet leave them as they were? What wives, daughters, sisters, did they in fine make credible; and what, in especial, was the speech, what the manners, what the general dietary, what most the monstrous morning meal, of ladies receiving at such hands the law or the license of life?" *(AS,* p. 426).

I would argue that James's international fiction concerns itself with depicting, among other things, the "speech" and the "manners," if not always the "general dietary," of the young American woman who is the daughter and sister of such men. But of course that fiction also, more seriously, depicts the psychology that James felt might result from a woman's living in such a situation. For, as he imagines the "exposed maiden" crying, "How can I do *all* the grace, *all* the interest, as I'm expected to?—yes, literally all the interest that isn't the mere interest on the money. I'm expected to supply it all—while I wander and stray in the desert" *(AS,* p. 431). If, then, James's fictional American heroines experience extreme difficulty in withstanding "the whole assault of life," that is perhaps the result of their cultural heritage, of their having been, like the exposed maidens of *The American Scene*, "too long abandoned and too *much* betrayed" *(AS*, p. 432).

2

The Psychology of the International Drama and the Requirements of Its Heroine

We seem at moments to see the incoherence and volatility of childhood, its living but in the sense of its hour and in the immediacy of its want, its instinctive refusal to be brought to book, its boundless liability to contagion and boundless incapacity for attention, its ingenuous blankness to-day over the appetites and clamours of yesterday, its chronic state of besprinklement with the sawdust of its ripped-up dolls, which it scarce goes even through the form of shaking out of its hair—we seem at moments to see these things, I say, twinkle in the very air, as by reflection of the movement of a great sunny playroom floor. The immensity of the native accommodation, socially speaking, for the childish life, is not that exactly the key of much of the spectacle?—the safety of the vast flat expanse where every margin abounds and nothing too untoward need happen.

—The American Scene

I

If James was distressed by the ways in which America was being blighted, his horror must surely have been intensified, given another turn of the screw, by his sense that those inflicting the damage were, in all senses but the physical, mere children. Throughout *The American Scene* he notes his impression that America reflected "the incoherence and volatility of childhood" *(AS,* p. 171), a condition which kept Americans themselves, he wrote in the Preface to *The Reverberator,* utterly "unaware" and which led them, when they visited Europe, to treat it "as a vast painted and gilded holiday toy" *(AN,* p. 189). James clearly found this "native accommodation . . . for the childish life" both puzzling and exasperating. At the same time, however, it constituted a condition of American life which provided him with some of his richest material. And it also provided the initial sensibility for the central actor of the international drama, the American girl.

Any perusal of James's international fiction—both the short fiction and the long, both the early and the late—impresses upon the reader a sense of the remarkable fascination with which James regarded its primary situation. The youthful, innocent, unaware American girl arriving on the European scene quite clearly constitutes an enormously significant moment for James. The seriousness with which he handles this moment varies from fiction to fiction, of course, but it is quite obvious that more than differences in manners and customs is at stake. This international drama has been and can be characterized by various formulae, including variations on the early description offered by Ferner Nuhn: "Europe is form without spirit, America is spirit without form."[1] My interest in this study in the psychological character of the principal figure in the international drama suggests that a psychological approach to the drama itself might be fruitful. For if James's interest in his heroine lies in the degree to which she is psychologically prepared to confront the European experience, then certainly the drama itself might be a configuration of certain fundamental and universal human experiences. For this reason, our understanding of James's international drama and of the American girl at its center can be enlarged by examining it from the perspective offered by contemporary theories of human psychology.

Among the most significant theorists currently advancing our understanding of human psychology, the Freudian revisionist Jacques Lacan provides insights and approaches that are especially amenable to literary analysis. Studying closely Freud's works, especially those on the unconscious and on narcissism, Lacan and others have shown that traditional ideas about a unified, controlled, integrated self must be wholly rethought and even renounced. We must recognize instead that human beings are essentially beings in discord who continually seek to create a sense of harmony by constructing "unified egos" which are in fact imaginary. These ideas will be of particular relevance to my examination of the principal American heroines, Isabel Archer, Milly Theale, and Maggie Verver. Of immediate use to my discussion of the international drama itself are some of Lacan's theories about the early development of the child.

Lacan, like Freud, assumes that the primary experiences of childhood constitute the paradigms that will dictate all subsequent experiences of the adult.[2] As Freud recognized, we continually repeat the experiences of earliest infancy. Lacan theorizes that the most important of our early experiences is that by which we first come to distinguish ourselves from the rest of the world. The child's discovery of this distinction is made possible by the periodic absences of the mother,[3] which constitute a "lack of object" to the child. Before this discovery, Lacan argues, the child has been at one with, inseparable from, the world. By contrast, the experience of "lack of object" is "what enables the child to progress to the subjectivity of 'I.'"[4] The very experience of a subjective "I" is therefore based on an experience of a divided reality and for this reason it is an uncomfortable, perturbing experience. It is also what leads to desire, sexuality, which likewise, in the words of Shoshana Felman, *"is the division and divisiveness of meaning."*[5] What distinguishes humans as humans, then, is precisely their desire to achieve unity and "non-difference" once again, but this desire is also, of course, a desire for annihilation. Human desire is thus ultimately and inevitably doomed to frustration.

Lacan seems to imply, then, that to be fully human is to choose to exist within the subjective "I," that is, to accept the ambiguity and ambivalence of a divided reality; to be fully human is also to accept that a whole or unified "self" is not possible. There is, of course, a strong resistance on the part of the individual to the experience of the subjective "I," and this resistance is essentially a suicidal impulse. The struggle to live within the subjective "I" is thus a struggle *for* life, *against* death.

The initial experience of "lack of object" on the part of the infant is an experience repeated throughout life. And because it is an experience that leads the infant to perceive *difference* for the first time, all subsequent experiences of difference will similarly propel the individual into the subjective "I." One form of resistance to the recognition of difference between self and Other (and, for Lacan, the Other is within the self as well as outside it) is identification with the Other. Through the process of identification the individual attempts once more to eliminate difference, division. In desiring to *be* the Other, the individual again "ultimately seeks the annihilation of the other as an independent subject."[6] The complexity involved in identification may, of course, result in much more ambiguous expressions than this. In particular, Lacan uses Hegel's dialectics of the *belle âme* to show how the individual may experience fear of the Other "because he wants so much to be the other, but being the other means losing himself."[7] Again, the *belle âme* cannot tolerate an ambiguous, ambivalent reality.

James's international fiction poses to the American girl the challenge that Lacan argues is fundamental: the challenge to become a subjective "I," accepting all the uncertainty and ambivalence attendant upon that state. In many of the international dramas James explores the various kinds of resistance brought by the American girl to acknowledging such a subjective "I."

One could of course object that James's international fiction is not necessarily unique in figuring forth this fundamental situation. But the point is that in his particular vision of Americans as childlike, unaware human beings, coming to Europe to learn something of "life," James came upon the perfect metaphor for this most basic of human situations. The literal foreignness of the Other, the subsequent threat this forcignness brings to the American girl by challenging her, for the first time perhaps, to become a subjective "I," to discard her psychological as well as her cultural provincialism—we can see how these elements could give a radically new content to a form that is timeless.

The American girl's encounter with the Otherness of Europe forces her for the first time to recognize the world as divided, as ambiguous. As we will see, the responses of James's heroines vary greatly. In some of the early fiction, the girl steadfastly keeps her eyes closed to the Other. In the novels, the girl encounters an Other who she in some ways longs to be— Isabel Archer meets Madame Merle; Milly Theale meets Kate Croy; Maggie Verver meets Charlotte Stant—and we see a variety of responses to the temptation held out by identification. Whatever the response, however, I believe that James equates the withstanding of the whole assault of life with the withstanding of the uncertain experience of the subjective "I." But as I will try to show in the following pages, the American girl's ability to achieve this sort of identity is to no small extent diminished or weakened by the fact that she is an American woman. To exist as a subject—to be an agent of action rather than simply a receiver or object of action—was difficult if not impossible for any woman of the nineteenth century. And, as an analysis of *The American Scene* suggests, it was particularly problematic for an American woman.

II

The difficulties in an American woman's benefiting from her confrontation with the Other are explored by James in much of the early international fiction, fiction that tends to center itself outside the heroine's consciousness. Such an exploration is evident, in fact, in James's first presentation of the American girl in Europe, the *nouvelle* "Madame de Mauves," written in 1874. The heroine of this story, Euphemia de Mauves, is—as her subsequent fictional sisters will nearly always be—a wealthy and innocent American girl, and she marries an impoverished but aristocratic Frenchman. James isolates in Euphemia's character a quality that looks forward to the more complex Isabel Archer, namely, Euphemia's idealism.[8] Madame de Mauves' idealism assumes a particular slant: she determines while she is still a young girl to marry a man who "should have 'race' in a state as documented as it was possible to have it" because "she had a romantic belief that the enjoyment of inherited and transmitted consideration attached to the fact of birth, would be the direct guarantee of an ideal delicacy of feeling" (XIII, 226, 224).[9] James's primary interest in his depiction of Euphemia de Mauves does not lie, of course, in the particular ideal she attempts to realize but rather in her inability to alter her ideal in accord with reality: "Even after experience had given her a hundred rude hints she found it easier to believe in fables, when they had a certain nobleness of meaning, than in well-attested but sordid facts" (XIII, 224-25).

If for James's final American girl, Maggie Verver, "knowledge is a fascination and a fear" (XXIV, 140), for Euphemia de Mauves it is only a "fear." Her fear of knowledge becomes, moreover, a defining characteristic of James's other American girls; and the pain and suffering attendant upon knowledge are what make Euphemia "a person who's begging off from full knowledge," a person who wishes to live "with closed eyes" (XIII, 268). Although readers of this story have generally, and rightly, emphasized the unyielding puritan qualities of Euphemia de Mauves, the story also suggests that Euphemia's fear of the pain accompanying knowledge, rather than her commitment to her ideal itself, motivates her behavior.[10] As she explains to Longmore, "I'm a dreadful coward about having to suffer or to bleed. I've always tried to believe that—without base concessions—such extremities may always somehow be dodged or indefinitely postponed. I should be willing to buy myself off, from having ever to be *overwhelmed*, by giving up—well, any amusement you like" (XIII, 257).

In Lacan's terms, Euphemia prefers not to open her eyes to the Other—to knowledge—because in so doing she would be forced into the uncomfortable experience of division and difference. The fear of knowledge is also, Lacan would argue, a fear of love, and this of course is particularly relevant to Madame de Mauves, who cannot love her husband precisely because he proves so different from her expectations. The extreme fear of "suffering" and "bleeding" expressed by Euphemia de Mauves becomes an important feature of James's other American girls; it later prompts Isabel Archer, Milly Theale, and Maggie Verver to attempt, like Euphemia de Mauves, to "dodge or indefinitely postpone" knowledge. If, in fact, a fear of the suffering accompanying knowledge or "awareness" makes Americans in general and the American girl in particular unnaturally prolong their blissful state of unawareness, then the trauma the American girl experiences when she is invited to eat of "the tree of knowledge" which she finds in Europe perhaps becomes more explicable.

Mary Garland, the American girl of the novel James himself designated his first, *Roderick Hudson*, discusses at one point the particular kind of suffering brought about by the knowledge and experience represented in James's international scheme by Europe. To embrace that knowledge and experience means, she explains, "to break with the past—I mean with one's poor old own. And breaking's a pain" (I, 333). The qualities which characterize Europe represent a threat to this young American innocent: "'Immemorial, complex, accumulated'—ah, those are words I'm afraid of" (I, 334). Mary Garland perfectly comprehends the implications of these words, but, unlike Euphemia de Mauves, she has a capacity, despite her fears, to respond: "I used to think . . . that if any trouble came to me I should bear it like a stoic. But that was at home, where things don't speak to us of enjoyment as they do here. Here it's such a mixture; one doesn't know what to choose, what to believe. . . . This place has destroyed any scrap of consistency that I ever possessed, but even if I must myself say something sinful I love it!" (I, 457).

The "mixture" of good and evil which complicates "what to choose, what to believe" seems to create a large measure of the fear of knowledge—and, by implication, the fear of experience and ultimately of life itself—that characterizes James's American girls. Many learn to develop, like Bessie Alden of "An International Episode" (1878-79), a "beautiful system, of consenting to know nothing of human baseness or of the vulgar side. There were things, just as there were people, that were as nought from the moment one ignored them" (XIV, 367).

Several of these American girls of the short fiction have, of course, no need to put on blinders because the blinders seem to be a part of their native equipment. Such is the case with James's most famous American girl, Daisy Miller, who was, he said in a letter, "too ignorant, too irreflective, too little versed in the proportions of things" to be able to take "the measure really of the scandal she produced."[1] It is likewise the case of Miranda Hope in one of James's less familiar tales, "A Bundle of Letters" (1879): "She looks at everything, goes everywhere, passes her way with her clear quiet eyes wide open; skirting the edge of obscene abysses without suspecting them; pushing through brambles without tearing her robe; exciting, without knowing it, the most injurious suspicions; and always holding her course—without a strain, without a sense, without a fear" (XIV, 502). This kind of total unawareness, the dominant characteristic of such American girls as Daisy Miller, Miranda Hope, and Sophy Ruck, has its roots in certain qualities of American life; as Miss Sturdy observes in "The Point of View" (1882), "the country's made for the rising generation; life's arranged for them," and as a consequence, "the girls aren't shy, but I don't know why they should be, for there's really nothing here to be afraid of" (XIV, 564-65). The Daisys and Mirandas were, as James says in the Preface to *The*

Reverberator, "unprecedented creatures" who, "conscious of so few things in the world . . . were least of all conscious of deficiencies and dangers" *(AN,* p. 188). Their position, like Lily Gunton's in "Miss Gunton of Poughkeepsie" (1900), is simply "that of being extraordinarily pretty, amazingly free, and perplexingly good" (XIV, 374).

James's full-scale treatment of the American girl in the novels does not, of course, posit the kind of total unawareness and unconsciousness exhibited by Daisy Miller. Although Isabel Archer, Milly Theale, and Maggie Verver respond variously to the "deficiencies and dangers" they encounter, they are able and willing at least to open their eyes and see them. So, too, are many of the American girls of the short fiction. Indeed, although an initially unsuspecting and completely blind innocence (what Lacan would call asubjectivity) constitutes a salient feature of James's American girl, it cannot exclusively define her character—as is the case with Daisy Miller—if she is to serve as the central figure of any long fiction; as James remarks in the Preface to *The Princess Casamassima,* "the person capable of feeling in the given case more than another of what is to be felt for it . . . is the only sort of person on whom we can count not to betray, to cheapen or, as we say, give away, the value and beauty of the thing" *(AN,* p. 67). Thus, the narrator of "The Pension Beaurepas" (1879) explains that although "there are plenty of" blank and blind American girls (like Sophy Ruck of this story and like Daisy Miller), "there are other forms" the American girl takes (XIV, 462). James's own interest lay, clearly, with these "other forms" of the American girl.[12]

In his study of James's New England girls, Eakin argues that the crucial "other form" was the American girl possessed of an imagination,[13] one capable of transcending her native insensibility, and it is interesting to note that James uses a familiar convention of the novel to identify these imaginative American girls. Such wholly unaware creatures as Daisy Miller and Sophy Ruck are almost always obviously and even exceedingly pretty, which is generally not the case of those American girls with an imaginative capacity—including Isabel, Milly, and Maggie.[14] These American girls are apt to

possess, like Mary Garland of *Roderick Hudson,* a physical
beauty apparent only to people of intelligence: "She'll not be
thought pretty by people in general and desecrated as she
passes by the stare of every vile wretch who chooses to thrust
his nose under her bonnet; but a certain number of intelligent
people will find it one of the delightful things of life to look at
her" (I, 379).

A beauty that requires for its recognition an imaginative
inner eye in the beholder signals that it is the interior qualities
of the American girl that should claim our attention.[15] And
this "form" of the American girl becomes the dominant one in
James's international fiction. Such early heroines as
Euphemia de Mauves and Mary Garland, like the later Milly
Theale and Maggie Verver, possess the innocence of Daisy
Miller, but they possess as well a capacity at least to recognize
the Other even if they are not always able to live conscious of
that difference. They possess, like Daisy, the American
temperament, but they are not, like Daisy, wholly bound by
that temperament. James describes the essence of this form of
the American girl in a sketch for a play that he recorded in the
Notebooks; the heroine of his projected drama would be, he
said, "intensely American in temperament—with her
freedoms, her immunity from traditions, superstitions, fears
and *riguardi,* but with an imagination kindling with her new
contact with the presence of a *past,* a continuity, etc."[16]

The "immunity" from "fears" which James in this
passage—and in many other places—describes as part of the
American temperament becomes, in fact, one of the
immunities often lost by those American girls of "kindling"
imagination. Fear of knowledge, in particular, figures as an
important element of the psychology of Isabel Archer, Milly
Theale, and Maggie Verver. The capacity for consciousness
seems, paradoxically, intimately connected to the capacity for
fear in James's treatment of the American girl; exactly the
incapacity for fear distinguishes a Daisy Miller, for example,
from an Isabel Archer or a Milly Theale. Lacan would argue
that there can be no fear, just as there can be no subjective "I,"
until there is a perceived difference; fear is thus sometimes a
necessary element of growth and change. James himself, in

some of his late nonfiction, wrote at length about this apparent riddle. After his visit to America in 1904-5, James wrote two essays which were serialized in *Harper's Bazar,* "The Speech of American Women" and "The Manners of American Women." In the first of these he writes of the American woman that "the conditions of American life in general, and our great scheme of social equality in particular, have done many things for her, and left many others undone; but they have above all secured her this primary benefit that she is the woman in the world who is least 'afraid.'"[17] Her total lack of fear became for her, moreover, "her one great sign," the sign by which Europe "knew her."[18] Yet this sign, James argues, ultimately portends the doom of civilization, particularly in America where civilization depends so exclusively on the American woman. Civilization, James says, can flourish only if one can recognize and fear the possibility of losing it; thus, fear "often accompanies . . . high civility" and even "indeed appears more or less directly to guarantee" it.[19] His final appeal in the second essay, "The Manners of American Women," is that the American woman replace "the old theory of her having, in her native air, nothing to fear by the perception, so urgent now, that she has almost everything"—everything being simply the loss of civilization itself.[20]

James turned away from the unafraid Daisy Millers to the frequently fearful Isabel Archers because the American girl's ability to grasp the significance of the European experience— and, in James's mind, the significance of human life itself— depended on her capacity to see possible "abysses" and thereby, of course, to become afraid of falling into them. The focus of much of this study will be on how the major American girls respond to their glimpses of abysses and handle the fears aroused by walking near them. For it is clear from arguments in *The American Scene,* "The Speech of American Women," and "The Manners of American Women" that James felt American civilization itself was at stake in the behavior and attitude of the American woman. The psychology of his fictional American girls, created by the conditions of American life, suggests, however, the extremity of America's situation; for America's expectation that these "exposed maidens" should "supply all" the civilization even while they have "been too long abandoned and too *much* betrayed," is doomed to disappointment. And the girl herself, in the meanwhile, has been "practically lost" *(AS,* pp. 431-32).

3

The Impact of the American Male: The Short Fiction and *The American*

This opens up—or se rattache to—the whole subject, or question, about which Godkin, as I remember, one day last summer talked to me very emphatically and interestingly—the growing divorce between the American woman (with her comparative leisure, culture, grace, social instincts, artistic ambitions) and the male American immersed in the ferocity of business, with no time for any but the most sordid interests, purely commercial, professional, democratic and political. This divorce is rapidly becoming a gulf—an abyss of inequality, the like of which has never before been seen under the sun. One might represent it, picture it, in a series of illustrations, of episodes—one might project a lot of light upon it. It would abound in developments, in ramifications.

—Notebook *entry, 26 November 1892*

I

As we saw in *The American Scene* and as James recorded in the *Notebook* entry above, there was in the latter part of the nineteenth century a "growing divorce between the American woman . . . and the male American." As the *Notebook* entry also indicates, the "abyss of inequality" resulting from this divorce provided James the novelist with an artistic gold mine because that abyss abounded "in developments, in ramifications." Much of James's short international fiction is devoted precisely to one of these, which he describes in another *Notebook* entry as the fact that America characteristically presented itself to Europe in the figure of "the manless American woman."[1] Thus, for example, Daisy Miller's father, in the words of little Randolph, "ain't in Europe—he's in a better place than Europe . . . [he's] in Schenectady. He's got a big business" (XVIII, 13). Similarly, Lily Gunton's only relation is "a grandfather carrying on a business in an American city" (XVI, 374), and although Violet Ray (of "A Bundle of Letters") arrives in Paris with both father and mother, she is soon happily disburdened of her father, who returns to America to tend to business. Miranda Hope, of the same story, naively believes that her travel alone in Europe constitutes a reasonable state of affairs: "I've discovered none of those objections to a young lady travelling in Europe by herself of which we heard so much before I left, and I don't expect I ever shall, for I certainly don't mean to look for them" (XIV, 481). In "An International Episode" James humorously depicts Bessie Alden's brother-in-law, Mr. Westgate, as consistently "confined to New York" by his business; and when Bessie and Mrs. Westgate travel to Europe, they go without Mr. Westgate, a fact to which his wife has learned to resign herself: "To the lost comfort of a husband respectably to produce, as she phrased it, she was now habituated; she had made half a dozen journeys to Europe under this drawback of

42

looking ill-temperedly separated and yet of being thanklessly enslaved" (XIV, 331).

In these tales and others as well, the American girl (and, if she has one, her mother) tends to think of the American male almost exclusively as the provider of the money she spends. Thus, for example, Lily Gunton's communication with her grandfather "was all by cable and on the subject of 'drawing'" (XVI, 374). The American male in James's fiction, wholly absorbed in the accumulation of money, launches the American girl in Europe as attestation of his own success, and there can be little beyond an economic bond between them. In some instances this economic bond creates in the American girl a passion for consumption—and sometimes this is her only passion.[2] Violet Ray resents her father's "theory that we're always running-up bills, whereas a little observation would show him that we wear the same old *rags* FOR MONTHS" (XIV, 490). And Sophy Ruck, of "The Pension Beaurepas," spends all of her time buying clothes and jewelry; her "jaded faded" father, one of James's few sympathetically treated businessmen, comforts himself by habitually observing that this "buying" constitutes "the principal interest for ladies" (XIV, 412)—and the implications of the language he uses are telling. But if, as the narrator of this story explains, "the duty of an American husband and father is to keep" his wife and daughter "going" (XIV, 461), James suggests that the callous indifference to anything but buying demonstrated by Sophy Ruck and other American girls is in fact the logical result of "their weak-kneed sire and his 'absorption in business'" (XIV, 462).

These "indulged ladies" of the American businessman (*AS*, p. 455), having mastered only the art of spending money, are often, like Sophy Ruck, "remarkably independent of most of the usual feminine aids to idleness—light literature, tapestry, the use of the piano" (XIV, 414). Sometimes James makes the connection between these deficiencies in the American girl and her businessman-father quite explicit. In *The Reverberator*, for example, Francie Dosson's "inconceivabilities of ignorance" (XIII, 16), which lead to her naive participation in George Flack's scandalous publication of the private lives of the Probert family, seem to be directly linked to her relationship with her father, who "had no tastes, no acquirements, no curiosities," and whose "daughters represented all society for him" (XIII, 21). In a description of Mr. Dosson that anticipates the later characterization of Adam Verver, James pinpoints the American girl's status in the eyes of the American male: "He thought much more and much oftener of these young ladies [his daughters] than of his bank-shares and railway-stock; they crowned much more his sense of accumulated property" (XIII, 21).[3] An ornament testifying to the American businessman's success, the American girl often feels herself, as Francie Dosson does, to be a frail, ineffectual creature: "She was not to be counted on; she was a vague soft negative being who had never decided anything and never would" (XIII, 58).

Not all of James's American girls, of course, are "vague soft negative" beings, but even those who are accorded the status of complex heroines do experience difficulty in encountering successfully the European experience and in achieving an identity. The particular characteristics of these heroines of the short fiction suggest that this difficulty perhaps results from the peculiar relationship they have with their fathers. Never having been real subjects in the world, many of them, like Francie Dosson, have "never decided anything and never" will. Moreover, the fact that their only passion is frequently a passion for spending their fathers' money would seem closely connected to the fact that they are also often, in the words of the aesthete Louis Leverett of "A Bundle of Letters," "slim" and "sexless" (XIV, 501). One of the more striking characteristics of all the American girls is just this sexlessness which they project, and this fact cannot, I think, be attributed to the often-exaggerated prudishness of James. The fiction itself attests that he sees the American girl's sexlessness as symbolic of her girlhood status. She has not yet become fully human, but is, rather, arrested in her psychosexual development.[4] Many of the American girls, like Daisy Miller, remain unawakened by the European experience, and consequently unaware of their sexuality. Others who do respond to the European experience, who recognize the

Otherness of Europe, are awakened in every sense, including the sexual. Their responses to this newly discovered sexuality vary, although the initial response seems often to be fear, as we will see particularly in the cases of Isabel Archer and Milly Theale.

Those heroines who remain unawakened by the European experience frequently manifest an inability to recognize the sexual implications of their flirtatious behavior—such blindness is present, for instance, in Daisy Miller, Sophy Ruck, and Francie Dosson. And this blindness to sexuality seems almost certainly related to the purely economic bond between the sexes in American life. Living symbols of father's business success, and spenders of his money, these American girls tend to project a "market" mentality onto the world in general; they treat male-female relations as a mechanical game, the gestures of which mean nothing. Thus, for example, Sophy Ruck's "conception of social intercourse appeared to consist of the imputation to as many persons as possible—that is to as many subject males—of some scandalous neglect of her charms and her claims" (XIV, 442). The American girl's "flirtatious" methods reduce "social intercourse" to the same kind of marketplace interaction that characterizes the American businessman's view of the world and that is the defining feature of male-female relations in America. Such a conception of "social intercourse" essentially dehumanizes both the girl and the men on whom she imposes it, including prospective suitors; Lily Gunton, for instance, requires her fiance to want her "more than anything else in the world" or she will not "want him" (XVI, 376).

Many of the American girls of James's short fiction can, then, conceive of male-female interactions only as a verbal repartee in which language is divorced from both human emotion and human behavior. Sexual passion—their own as well as that of the men they encounter—remains hidden and unknown. Again, this fact seems intimately linked to the conditions of American society as James perceived and recorded them. As we saw in *The American Scene*, the "universal law" which everywhere else has resulted in the mutual participation of men and women in the creation and

preservation of civilization has in America been successfully
ruptured *(AS,* p. 346). Except when they are very young, the
men are simply absent from the social scene. And, as Mrs.
Church observes in "The Point of View," the interactions of
young American men and young American girls are virtually
meaningless: "There's a peculiar custom in this country—I
shouldn't know how to express it in Genevese: it's called
'being attentive,' and young girls are the object of the futile
process. It hasn't necessarily anything to do with projects of
marriage—though it's the privilege only of the unmarried and
though at the same time . . . it has no relation to other projects.
It's simply an invention by which young persons of the two
sexes pass large parts of their time together with no questions
asked" (XIV, 556).

In a very real sense, then, some of the American girls—Daisy
Miller, Sophy Ruck, Francie Dosson, Bessie Alden—are truly
"slim" and "sexless." They have been unnaturally encouraged
by the conditions of American life that produced them to
remain in a state of perpetual girlhood. Their inability to
perceive their own sexuality can lead, as James suggests in the
case of Daisy Miller, to their destruction on the European
stage. But most of these heroines do not suffer such extreme
consequences; James simply notes their sexlessness as a
peculiar facet of their personality. The more serious
consequences which the American girl's psychosexual
development can create appear, James suggests, when the girl
does in fact awaken to her sexual identity. Characteristically,
as we will see especially in Milly Theale, this awakening
evokes in the girl a response of extreme fear; she experiences it
often as a threat to her total identity. Although only in the
novels does James fully depict this, we sometimes see hints of
it in the short fiction. Thus, for example, Gertrude Wentworth
looks forward to Isabel Archer in the response she has when
she senses that the Reverend Mr. Brand is going to propose to
her: "She felt . . . that what he meant had now a renewed
power to disturb her, to perplex and agitate her."[5] Similarly,
the kind of knowledge Euphemia de Mauves attempts to shun
has a decidedly sexual cast; she is "an American girl born
neither to submit basely nor to rebel crookedly marrying a

shining sinful Frenchman who believes a woman must do one or the other of those things" (XIII, 222). And significantly, her "shining sinful" husband's corruption, for which she unyieldingly refuses to forgive him, is a propensity to establish sexual relations with other women. Madame de Mauves thus moves from being a young American girl wholly unaware of sexual passion to being a wife determined to protect herself from its contaminating powers.

If the American girl's sexlessness makes it possible for the American man to idealize her as the essence of innocence and moral value (which is Longmore's view of Euphemia de Mauves), it also reflects the inability of the girl herself to become fully human. Moreover, the persistence with which the American male attempts to maintain the American girl as a beautiful object in his world suggests, once again, that the girl's inability to become fully human is promoted by the American male and his desires. For though the American girl may spend the money her father labors to produce, the production of the money is in fact the only valued activity; the only "interest" about which the American male seems to know or care is, as we have seen in *The American Scene*, "the mere interest on the money" *(AS*, p. 431). Furthermore, since the American girl has no sphere in which to create material achievements, she can gauge her worth only on the basis of the responses she receives from others; and since she receives, in essence, only a bank check from "the deep American man," she understandably often remains unawakened, fails to achieve a fully human status.

II

The failed attempt to achieve and maintain that status is the subject of a little-known tale first published by James in 1888 under the title "The Two Countries," and later renamed "The Modern Warning." The American girl of this tale, Agatha Grice, marries, against the violent disapproval of her patriotic brother, a British aristocrat. Macarthy Grice's disapproval of his sister's marriage has its ostensible base in his view that such a marriage is unpatriotic, "an abjuration, an apostasy, a kind of moral treachery."[6] Although Macarthy eventually accepts, with extreme reserve, Agatha's marriage to Sir Rufus Chasemore, a crisis develops within Agatha when she discovers that Sir Rufus plans to publish a book recording his negative impressions of the effects of democracy in America. Seeing his wife's acute distress over this book, however, Sir Rufus magnanimously volunteers to withhold the book from publication. A year later, after learning that her brother plans to visit her, Agatha inexplicably decides that this is too large a favor, that the book has literary merit, and that Sir Rufus should indeed publish it. Shortly thereafter, Macarthy Grice arrives in England only to discover that Agatha has that very day committed suicide.

Though "The Modern Warning" (which is also the title of Sir Rufus's book) does not rank among James's best international fiction, it does offer an interesting perspective on the relation of the American girl's psychology to the American man. Macarthy Grice's disapproval of Agatha's international marriage, and the effects of that disapproval on Agatha, are extreme, especially if we regard the issue as centering on Agatha's patriotism. But for both Macarthy and Agatha, her marriage to Sir Rufus constitutes not simply a cultural betrayal of America but, more importantly, a psychological betrayal of her brother. To their mother, Macarthy initially argues that "of course Agatha will marry some day; but why need she marry in such a way as to make a gulf?" (p. 30). But to himself Macarthy acknowledges that "he was so fond of his sister that he had a secret hope that she would never marry at all. He had spoken otherwise to his mother, because that was the only way not to seem offensively selfish; but the essence of his thought was that on the day Agatha should marry she would throw him over" (p. 32). Macarthy, like the much later Adam Verver, wants Agatha to remain perpetually single—and thereby, of course, a perpetual "girl"—because he does not wish her to form a life separate from his own; instead, she should remain attached to him because "his mother and his sister *were* his home" (p. 31). Agatha's responsibility to him simply increases after their mother dies, and she accordingly feels acute guilt that she has abandoned him by marrying Sir Rufus: "Lady Chasemore was prepared to feel pang upon pang when she should perceive how much less comfortably he lived than he would have lived if she had not quitted him" (p. 48).

Macarthy himself is totally—and excessively, the story suggests—devoted to his business, and uninterested in marriage for himself, a fact to which Agatha occasionally attaches particular significance: "It sometimes seems to me as if he didn't marry on purpose to make me feel badly" (p. 47). And certainly his single life has resulted in a state of affairs that operates to make Agatha "feel badly" and that also points to the primary reasons for marriage in America: "her brother's life struck her as bare, ungarnished, helpless, socially and domestically speaking" (p. 48). Macarthy Grice's conception, then, of his sister's duty—a conception she herself to some extent shares—is that she should live with him, in perpetual girlhood, and manage his social and domestic life for him. His own desire to remain single suggests that he can really conceive of no greater need for women in his life than that which his sister could fulfill. His wife is his business.

Agatha initially, before she marries Sir Rufus, accepts Macarthy's notion that marrying an Englishman would constitute a betrayal of her American heritage: "If she were not careful she would give her country away: in the privacy of her own room she had coloured up to her hair at the thought" (p. 38). James, however, carefully emphasizes in the story that Macarthy and America are one, and that what Agatha is in danger of "giving away," by making a life of her own, is her brother. Similarly, her later protest against Sir Rufus's book stems not from her own patriotism but from her fear of Macarthy's reaction: "it was in a great degree the refiguration of her brother's cold, lifelong scorn that had ndled in her . . . the passion with which she now protested" . 75).

The psychological process by which Agatha comes to rse her position and to persuade Sir Rufus to publish his book reveals the extent to which she has been unable to claim, without guilt, an identity and a life separate from her brother's. During the months following Sir Rufus's promise to put away the book that was to represent his "signal service to his country" (p. 76), Agatha begins to doubt of the moral rightness of her position; she begins to believe that Sir Rufus "suffered and that he regarded himself as a kind of traitor" for not publishing his warning against democracy (p. 80). But this conviction "only ministered to the love she had ever borne him—the love that had had the power originally to throw her into his arms in the face of an opposing force. As month followed month all her nature centered itself in this feeling" (p. 80). Significantly, what seems to precipitate her decision to make Sir Rufus publish his book after all is a letter she receives from her brother, announcing his intention to visit her. Reading his letter gives Agatha "a vision of his reason for offering to let her see him in England; it was a piece of appreciation on Macarthy's part, a reward for their having behaved—that is, for Sir Rufus's having behaved, apparently under her influence—better than might have been expected. He had the good taste not to bring out his insolent book, and Macarthy gave this little sign, the most mollified thing he had done as yet, that he noticed" (p. 81). Agatha goes to tell her husband of Macarthy's approaching visit, but this news "held Sir Rufus's attention very briefly, and in a few minutes Agatha herself ceased to dwell upon it. Suddenly, illogically, fantastically, she could not have told why, at that moment and in that place, for she had had no such intention when she came into the room, she broke out: 'My own darling, do you know what has come over me? I have changed entirely—I see it differently; I want you to publish that grand thing'" (p. 81).

Although Agatha herself "could not have told why" she at this moment changes her mind about Sir Rufus's book, the chain of events leading up to that decision allows at least the reader to understand. For it has been in a state of renewed love for her husband that Agatha has received Macarthy's letter; and her interpretation of the letter makes her aware, on some level, of the power she has allowed Macarthy to exert over her and her marriage to Sir Rufus. Her subsequent outburst to her husband thus seems to represent her attempt to assert her own separateness from Macarthy, her own integrity. But her success in establishing an independent self proves to be, of course, virtually nonexistent. For although she courageously watches Sir Rufus resume preparations for the publication of his book, when the day of Macarthy's visit arrives, she proves unable to encounter him. Her one strong assertion of herself must be paid, at least in her mind, with her own life. There thus seems to be considerable truth in Sir Rufus's exclamation to Macarthy that "by God, you have killed her! it's your infernal work!" (p. 85). And the extent to which Macarthy himself has felt his sister to belong to him is vividly illustrated when "he rushed at his sister and for a moment almost had a struggle with her husband for the possession of her body, in which, as soon as he touched it, he felt the absence of life" (p. 85).

James's presentation of Agatha Grice in this story looks forward in important ways to Milly Theale and Maggie Verver. A confused or inadequate sense of self is, as we will see, Milly Theale's primary affliction in *The Wings of the Dove*, just as it is a primary affliction for Isabel Archer in *The Portrait of a Lady*. Among the causes of such an inadequate sense of self is, as both "The Modern Warning" and *The Golden Bowl* suggest, the American girl's relation to the American male, a relation which seems to result either in her inability to establish a separate self or, if she attempts to establish one, in extreme guilt. Agatha Grice's fear of "betraying" her brother by daring to shape a life for herself anticipates Maggie Verver's similar fear of "betraying" her father in *The Golden Bowl*.[7] Although James ends "The Modern Warning" with uncharacteristic melodrama, the tale nevertheless clearly suggests both the American girl's excessive fear of becoming a subjective "I" and the role of the American male in creating or contributing to that fear.

III

Further understanding of the ways in which male-female relationships in America contribute to the American girl's deep sense of an inner inadequacy may be gained from a consideration of James's first international novel, *The*

American, initially serialized in *The Atlantic Monthly* during the period June 1876-May 1877. Despite the fact that this novel does not use the figure of the American girl, the masculine-feminine conflict it dramatizes seems directly analogous to the relationship between the sexes that figures so prominently in the distinctive psychology of the American girl; it is thus not surprising that Banta has recently noted a similarity in "moods and motifs" between *The American* and *The American Scene.*[8]

The American is, of course, primarily a comedy of manners that depicts the innocent American, Christopher Newman, confounded by the traditions of the aristocratic Bellegardes, whose daughter he wishes to marry. This daughter, Claire de Cintré, receives only minor development in the novel, and her somewhat melodramatic decision at the end of the novel to renounce both Newman and the world by becoming a Carmelite nun is, as James acknowledges in the Preface, seemingly inexplicable: "The delicate clue to her conduct is never definitely placed in his [the reader's] hand" *(AN,* p. 39). Thus, both because Madame de Cintré's decision to enter the convent "for life" is inadequately explained, and because a full development of her character is sacrificed in the novel to the more important focus on Newman *(AN,* pp. 38-39), critics of the novel have been understandably reluctant to view her renunciatory gesture as having any causal connections with Newman's character or behavior.[9] Claire de Cintré herself has remained somewhat peripheral to critical discussions of the novel, which, following James's own focus in the Preface, have tended to center instead on Newman and on the response to him of old Madame de Bellegarde and her son, Urbain. In refusing Newman, most critics have agreed, Claire is merely obeying her family's wishes; her further denial of life itself— her decision to become a Carmelite nun—is generally considered, if it is considered at all, as a gratuitous and extravagant gesture used by James to aid in the development of Newman's character. The major concerns of *The American* thus seem to have blurred, both for James and his readers, some of the possible reasons for and implications of Claire's decision to enter the convent. Claire herself emerges from critical discussions as a pawn caught between her family and Newman; as Daniel Schneider recently expressed this view, "in the end Claire enters the convent, refusing to accede either to her family or to the aggressive Newman. She cannot bear to side with one party against the other."[10]

There are, however, more complex causal connections between Newman's character and behavior and Claire's decision to enter the convent. The parallels which James establishes in the novel between Claire de Cintré and her younger brother, Valentin de Bellegarde, both of whom Newman regards as "feminine," provide an access to those connections and suggest that Claire's renunciatory gesture at the end of the novel in part represents her response to the character and the values of the American Newman. James, defending the novel's ending to his friend Howells, claimed that "it was cruelly hard for poor N. to lose, certainly; but . . . there are tall stone walls which fatally divide us. I have written my story from Newman's side of the wall, and I understand so well how Mme de Cintré couldn't really scramble over from *her* side!"[11] But both *The American* itself and James's other international fiction suggest that these "tall stone walls" do not result simply from cultural differences, for cultural barriers alone do not prevent many of James's American girls from marrying European men. The "tall stone walls" separating Newman and Claire de Cintré seem instead the result of Newman's aggressive and wholly materialistic masculinity. His character and behavior, in fact, perhaps help explain a phenomenon which baffled and intrigued James, namely the fact that the international marriage always involved the male European and "the female American—never the other way round."[12] Certainly, however, Newman's character and its effects on Claire de Cintré and Valentin de Bellegarde suggest some of the ways the psychology of the American girl may be related to the American man.

Christopher Newman is, of course, quintessentially masculine and American.[13] A fairy-tale, rags-to-riches hero, Newman is a businessman whose success has known no limits, and whose first word in the novel—"Combien?"— characterizes his general approach to life and his values, those which James believed to be typical of the American male. Newman's European experience centers on two relationships: his courtship of Claire de Cintré and his friendship with her younger brother, Valentin de Bellegarde. The brother and sister are remarkably close and strikingly similar; as Valentin de Bellegarde remarks, he and Madame de Cintré "are such a brother and sister as have not been since Orestes and Electra" (p. 105).[14] The brother and sister not only "strongly" resemble each other in appearance, as Newman himself notices (p. 43), but they also share an openness and a flexibility that sharply distinguish them from their mother and older brother. Newman himself responds to similar, if somewhat differently manifested, qualities within both Valentin and Claire. Significantly, while Newman is attracted to both of them by the same qualities—presented in the novel as essentially "feminine" qualities—he can prize and value those qualities only in Claire, not in her brother. Educated, cultured, graceful, and elegant, Valentin and Claire are both sources of pleasure to Newman, but because Valentin is a male, Newman's affection for him is inevitably mingled with pity. Thus, while such qualities lead Newman to regard Claire as a very desirable wife, they lead him to pity and disfavor Valentin. Claire challenges Newman about his attitude early in their courtship, accusing him of treating Valentin as he might treat a child, and concludes that though Valentin "amuses" Newman, Newman does not respect her brother (pp. 176-77). Later in the novel, Newman acknowledges to himself that "he had a sort of pity" for Valentin, and reveals that "it mortified him, moreover, to think that Valentin lacked money" (p. 235).

Writing from Newman's own perspective, Richard Poirier has argued that both Claire and Valentin are "imprisoned Americans, and Newman tries literally to set them both free."[15] Certainly Newman seeks to convert Valentin into an American businessman and Claire into an American wife—but the notion that they are "imprisoned Americans" is sharply questioned by the novel itself. More importantly, Newman's determination to "free" the brother and sister by making them conform to his own definitions of male and female has ultimately destructive effects upon both Valentin and Claire.

Valentin dies in the course of the novel, killed by a fatal gunshot wound incurred in a duel of honor. His decision to force the duel that results in his death occurs during an evening at the opera. The intermissions preceding his "quarrel" with the insolent M. Kapp are the occasions of two conversations with Newman, who tries to persuade him to come make his fortune in America. Prompted by feelings of pity for Valentin, Newman offers to "put" the younger man "through" by finding him a business position in America. Though Valentin maintains his characteristic ironic pose throughout the two conversations, he nevertheless seems to submit to being judged according to Newman's masculine American values of commercialism: "It would look as if I were a strong man, a first-rate man, a man who dominated circumstances" (p. 234). Later, he accedes, half-jokingly, to Newman's ambitious plans for him: "Well, then, put me through; push me in! I make myself over to you. Dip me into the pot and turn me into gold" (p. 236).

Two important ideas reverberate in Valentin's comments to Newman. The first is that Valentin has begun to share Newman's view of him as somehow deficient as a man, at least as "a strong man, a first-rate man." Second, the only way for him to correct this deficiency, in Newman's mind, is by becoming an American businessman, by pursuing the wealth which alone can validate his masculinity. Yet the irony inherent in Valentin's command that Newman "dip" him "into the pot" of gold and thereby transform him underscores Valentin's recognition that his achieving the material success Newman envisions for him is impossible because it would require a transformation of his total identity. James, through the extravagance of his metaphor, clearly criticizes the whole equation of masculinity with material success. The "freedom" to become an American, which Newman offers Valentin, is not only elusive for the Frenchman, but also reflects the least attractive aspect of Newman's own character. Newman's blind belief in the enormous virtue of commercialism points again to his representative status, from James's point of view, as an American man; as Leon Edel has pointed out, Newman represents "everything that Henry disliked in the United States," especially because he is an American "who is hospitable to life's chances, but who is 'committed to nothing in particular' save his own incredible self-assurance."[16]

Newman's "incredible self-assurance" makes him, of course, incapable of understanding the effect of his vision of reality and his patronizing attitude upon Valentin's sense of himself. To Newman there can be no connection between his offers to transform Valentin into an American businessman and Valentin's forcing of the quarrel with M. Kapp immediately after those offers. Yet the juxtaposition of the two scenes can hardly be accidental; because Valentin cannot become a "strong man, a first-rate man" through his transformation into an American businessman he feels forced to resort to a European concept of masculinity by committing himself to "the beautiful though somewhat superannuated image of honour" (p. 98). Early in the novel Valentin remarks that Newman makes "me feel as if I had missed something" (p. 97), and Newman's attempts to provide the "something" in this opera scene, a something predicated on his gospel of hope and his own image of masculinity, serve only to trigger Valentin's despair and to plunge him into the duel that results in his death.

Newman's visit to the dying Valentin symbolically reinforces this connection between Newman's attempts to Americanize and masculinize Valentin and Valentin's fatal duel, which is, like Claire's becoming a Carmelite nun, a "dusky old-world expedient" (p. 288). Newman asks the dying Valentin how he is "getting on," to which Valentin replies:

> "Oh, I'm getting off! They have quite settled that; haven't they?"
> "That's for you to settle; you can get well if you try," said Newman with resolute cheerfulness.
> "My dear fellow, how can I try? Trying is violent exercise, and that sort of thing isn't in order for a man with a hole in his side as big as your hat." (pp. 264-65)

The bantering tone of this conversation should neither mislead us about its seriousness nor deceive us about the depth of feeling the two men have for each other. But the language of the passage bears a more serious interpretation. Newman's remark that Valentin "can get well if" he tries reveals the specific assumptions Newman has made about Valentin—not here, on his deathbed, but earlier, before his duel. Valentin should have changed his life, since clearly he was not "well"; moreover, he could have changed his life had he wished, could have become a successful American businessman had he wished, because the only condition of such a transformation, from Newman's point of view, is his *will*. Valentin's reply also transcends the immediate circumstances of their conversation; it expresses his recognition of the impossibility of his becoming the kind of man Newman envisioned, and also asserts his understanding that something more than his *will* is involved. The hole in his side functions as an apt symbol of the fatal feeling of deficiency that Newman has succeeded in engendering in him. A short time later, Valentin pitifully remarks, "I am rather sorry about that place in the bank. Who knows but that I might have become another Rothschild? But I wasn't meant for a banker; bankers are not so easy to kill. Don't you think I have been very easy to kill? It's not like a serious man. It's really very mortifying" (pp. 267-68).

The "freedom" and "salvation" that Newman offers Valentin thus serve only to create in the younger man a "mortifying" sense of deficiency that leads to his death. Though Valentin had felt before he met Newman that his status as an aristocratic younger son was making him waste his life, the solution Newman proposes is no solution at all, involving as it does Valentin's rejection of his own values and of his ties to history, family, and social forms. To Newman those ties are unnecessary and even meaningless; and if they lead to individual unhappiness, they should—and can—be rejected. But Valentin recognizes that these ties are inescapable because they create identity; such ties help to define the self and therefore cannot easily be denied, even if they have undesirable effects. Newman's implicit devaluation of these ties, and of the "feminine" identity and values they have, in his mind, created, thus does not result in Valentin's severing the ties and creating a new identity—clearly, an impossibility; but it does result in Valentin's rejection of life itself, because

Valentin's life itself, ultimately, is what Newman has devalued.

If Valentin cannot have Newman's respect because he fails to conform to Newman's definition of what a man should do and be, his sister, because she is a woman, can receive from Newman only the kind of respect accorded other valuable possessions—the kind of respect the American man typically gives the American woman in James's fiction. As Susan P. Ward has observed, Claire is for Newman "all along like a great work of art which he must own,"[17] and there are numerous passages in the novel that confirm the idea that Claire is only an object to Newman. Like her real counterparts in America, Claire, as his wife, would figure to Newman as a kind of "embroidery" on his "canvas." To be sure, she is not a vulgar object, but "a very expensive article" (p. 117) for which Newman is willing to pay the highest price. And his perception of her as a maid in distress, whom he can rescue, simply adds to her value. It is not, however, Claire herself but rather her value as an object, a prized possession, that he respects.

This dehumanizing, materialistic attitude toward Claire has been frequently noted in critical discussions of Newman's character. It may also point, however, to that "light plank" over the "psychological abyss" of Claire's character, the absence of which has troubled both James and his readers (AN, p. 39). Early in their relationship, Claire warns Newman that "I have very little courage; I am not a heroine" (p. 152). Later, when she informs him of her decision to join the Carmelites, she protests that his idealized image of her "left me no loophole for escape—no chance to be the common weak creature I am" (p. 280). Little as Claire actually appears in the novel, little as we are given of the motives for her final decision, such evidence as this, coupled with the parallels between sister and brother, supports the notion that Newman's attitude toward her diminishes her sense of self worth and leads her into the convent. A conversation she has with Newman shortly before the Bellegardes' formal presentation of him to their friends provides convincing illustration of Newman's effect on Claire:

"If you only knew," he said, "how exactly you are what I coveted! And I am beginning to understand why I coveted it; the having it makes all the difference that I expected. Never was a man so pleased with his good fortune. You have been holding your head for a week past just as I wanted my wife to hold hers. You say just the things I want her to say. You walk about the room just as I want her to walk. You have just the taste in dress that I want her to have. In short, you come up to the mark; and, I can tell you, my mark was high."

These observations seemed to make Madame de Cintré rather grave. At last she said: "Depend upon it, I don't come up to the mark. Your mark is too high. I am not all that you suppose; I am a much smaller affair. She is a magnificent woman, your ideal. Pray, how did she come to such perfection?"

"She was never anything else," Newman said. (p. 210)

Though Claire's verbal response to Newman only protests that she is not the paragon that Newman thinks she is, her gravity might surely be a silent response to Newman's unwitting implication that she is a thing to be possessed. To realize that for Newman she is but an object, who walks and talks and dresses to his approval, would clearly be sufficient to make Madame de Cintré very grave indeed. Even more important, however, is the fact that Newman measures her, as he did Valentin, against an ideal that is alien to her. And she, like her brother, seems to fear that she is "a much smaller affair" who will prove unable to conform to Newman's standards. Thus, the fearful inadequacy Claire repeatedly expresses in the novel (an inadequacy experienced by such American girls as Isabel Archer and Milly Theale) would seem to be at least in part the result of Newman's expectations of and attitude toward her, and may provide one motive of her final rejection of both Newman and life itself. Like Valentin, who resorts to an old-world definition of masculinity by forcing a duel of honor, Claire, by entering the convent, resorts to an old-world definition of femininity. The brother and sister's need to rely on such life-denying measures as these reveals the extent to which their very identities have been threatened by Newman.

Though Mrs. Bread asserts that Claire has always been afraid, and that her fear is her only real fault, this fear has also been aggravated and worsened by Newman: "'She was afraid,' said Mrs. Bread, very confidently; 'she has always been afraid, or at least for a very long time. That was the trouble, sir. She was like a fair peach, I may say, with just one little speck. She had one little sad spot. You pushed her into the sunshine, sir, and it almost disappeared. Then they pulled her back into the shade and in a moment it began to spread. Before we knew it she was gone. She was a delicate creature'" (pp. 299-300). Mrs. Bread's comical metaphor here suggests another of Newman's serious effects on Claire; the "sunshine" of Newman makes Claire, the "fair peach," unable to withstand any longer the "shade" of her mother and older brother. The "darkness" of her family, which all her life Claire had been able to accept or tolerate without perishing, has been rendered intolerable by Newman's bright goodness. Newman, of course, proposes to rescue Claire from the "evil" which he perceives as inherent in her family and social situation. Claire recognizes that the "pull" of her family and social situation cannot be ignored, and yet Newman's attitude toward these makes it impossible for her to maintain her ties to her family without losing all sense of self worth. Her response is to reject life itself.

IV

Newman's opposed responses to the very similar Claire and Valentin suggest that the feminine civilized values embodied by the sister and brother may not be ultimately or inherently of real worth to Newman. Such values render Claire de Cintré a desirable possession—a desirable wife—but they reduce Valentin to an object of pity in need of salvation. Certainly Newman does try in the novel to transform his own money into more civilized forms, but his business mentality leads him to objectify and thereby seriously harm the people around him in the very process. As we have seen, a similar difficulty afflicts the relations between the American man and the American woman, leading, in James's later fiction, to similar effects on the American girl. James seemed further to recognize that a strong and confident sense of self cannot be developed if an individual understands that neither she, because she is a woman, nor her values, because they do not lead to monetary gain, are prized by her environment. As Karen Horney pointed out in the early 1920s, "our culture . . . is a male culture, and therefore by and large not favorable to the unfolding of woman and her individuality."[18] And the American girl's consistent difficulty in shaping a mature identity is a direct result of her inability to assert herself—an inability clearly arising from the conditions of life in America.

Yet she is, for James, a fascinating figure who embodies all his hopes as well as all his fears for America. As he develops the figure in *The Portrait of a Lady, The Wings of the Dove,* and *The Golden Bowl,* his interest consistently lies in her struggle to overcome, somehow, the crippling effects of her psychology. For James himself seemed to believe, like his sister Alice, that what "survives is the resistance we bring to life and not the strain life brings to us."[19] The same might be said of James's American girls: what survives in our memory of these fictional heroines is not the "strain" they encounter on the European stage, but the "resistance" they display in their dramas.

4

"Solutions" to "The Practical Problem of Life":
The Portrait of a Lady

Millions of presumptuous girls, intelligent or not intelligent, daily affront their destiny, and what is it open to their destiny to be, at the most, that we should make an ado about it? The novel is of its very nature an "ado," an ado about something, and the larger the form it takes the greater of course the ado. Therefore, consciously, that was what one was in for—for positively organising an ado about Isabel Archer.

—*Preface,* The Portrait of a Lady

I

James's preoccupation with the American girl in his early international fiction should have made it no surprise that his first full treatment of the figure coincided with his first major artistic achievement. As he wrote in a letter to Thomas Sergeant Perry, *The Portrait of a Lady* would be the novel from which "I myself shall pretend to date—on that I shall take my stand,"[1] and it is Isabel Archer, the American girl "affronting" her "destiny" in this novel, who largely justified James's confidence. For many readers, Isabel Archer and *The Portrait of a Lady* remain, in fact, James's most appealing American girl and his most admirable international novel. Isabel herself stands midway between the American girls of the early international fiction and those of the late fiction; while the complexity of her character looks forward to Milly Theale and Maggie Verver, the realistic methods James uses to reveal her character and experience in Europe closely connect her to such earlier girls as Daisy Miller and Bessie Alden. Isabel's continuing appeal to readers resides, it would seem, in her realistic dimensions. Like her predecessors, she is placed in a European external world of social relations; unlike many of them, however, she is endowed with a consciousness to some extent capable, at least in the later stages of her career, of understanding, judging, and accepting the conditions and values of that world. As James remarks in the Preface to the novel, Isabel's "adventures are to be mild"—like those of the earlier girls—but "her sense of them, her sense *for* them" gives them a significance missing from the adventures of the earlier American girls; the *Portrait* would show, then, "what an 'exciting' inward life may do for the person leading it even while it remains perfectly normal" *(AN,* pp. 56-57).

The central shift from the earlier international fiction to the *Portrait* involved the decision James made to center his novel in the consciousness of his American girl, rather than continuing to view her from the outside.[2] But this extraordinary reliance on "the single small cornerstone" that initially represented all his "outfit for the large building" of the novel *(AN,* p. 48) challenged James with new artistic difficulties. For although Isabel Archer was to be "complex," "intelligent," and even "presumptuous," and although she would possess a responsive imagination, these characteristics would not necessarily give her any greater possibilities than those open to many other girls, "intelligent or not intelligent." The challenge to James as a novelist thus involved "positively organising an ado" *(AN,* p. 48) about a character whose gender alone gave her a status so slender and options so limited as to make an "ado" seem nearly impossible.[3] Like "millions of presumptuous girls" who "daily affront" destinies severely limited by the social conditions of their time, Isabel Archer posed to James an "interesting," even "beautiful," artistic "difficulty" *(AN,* pp. 48, 51).

If, however, James brilliantly conquered this artistic difficulty by showing that the "inward life" of an ordinary woman could in fact serve as an "exciting" focus for the novel, he nevertheless seems to have confronted the limitations of realistic fiction as a mode for exploring the full potential of the American girl. For by placing this American girl in a novelistic world closely resembling the actual world of the 1870s, James was forced to focus not on the girl's latent potential for growth but on her actual dimensions. The conditions of Isabel Archer's world inevitably impinge upon her life and help determine the direction it can take. Thus, in the *Portrait* James reveals that his American girl is crippled, but not simply or exclusively by her own American-created psychology.[4] Many of Isabel's limitations result instead from James's determination to present a realistic portrait of a particular kind of nineteenth-century woman, and such a realistic portrait was determined in no small way by the conditions of the world the heroine inhabited. The social and economic restraints suffered by an ordinary woman of the nineteenth century are necessarily suffered by Isabel Archer, who is not, even after she inherits a fortune, an "heiress of all the ages." This fact perhaps helps explain why James's later American girls, Milly Theale and Maggie Verver, are freed of many of the external restraints on the individual—and particularly on the female individual; only through that freedom, moreover, does James seem able fully to explore the "deeper psychology"[5] of his American girl. Nevertheless, although Isabel Archer represents James's most realistically limited American girl, her own stature in accepting the limits of the possibilities open to her makes her also perhaps his most estimable vision of the American girl.

II

In the superbly ironic chapter which opens *The Portrait of a Lady,* Daniel Touchett, Isabel Archer's eventual fairy godfather, predicts, despite his own marital failure, that "the ladies will save us . . . that is the best of them will—for I make a difference between them" (III, 11). The immediate enthusiasm that Isabel Archer excites upon her arrival in England might well seem to justify old Mr. Touchett's belief in the redemptive power of "the ladies." Yet the central irony of the novel emerges from the discrepancy between the high expectations of Isabel held by her friends and herself and the actual powerlessness that inheres in her simply being a woman. Any estimate of Isabel's character must keep this fact in mind, must temper judgment with the steady realization of the ways in which James is using Isabel to explore the actual possibilities open to a woman of her day.[6] Indeed, contemporary readers of the *Portrait* viewed Isabel as typifying the condition of women; Horace E. Scudder, for example, reviewing the novel for *The Atlantic Monthly,* wrote: "The fine purpose of her freedom, the resolution with which she seeks to be the maker of her destiny, the subtle weakness into which all this betrays her, the apparent helplessness of her ultimate position, and the conjectured escape only through patient forebearance—what are all these, if not attributes of womanly life expended under current conditions?"[7]

The "current conditions" as they are established in the

novel take the form of the milieu in which James places his heroine, a milieu which, he says in the Preface to the novel, would answer for him the question of what his heroine would "do":

> I seem to myself to have waked up one morning in possession of them—of Ralph Touchett and his parents, of Madame Merle, of Gilbert Osmond and his daughter and his sister, of Lord Warburton, Caspar Goodwood and Miss Stackpole, the definite array of contributions to Isabel Archer's history. I recognised them, I knew them, they were the numbered pieces of my puzzle, the concrete terms of my "plot." It was as if they had simply, by an impulse of their own, floated into my ken, and all in response to my primary question: "Well, what will she do?" Their answer seemed to be that if I would trust them they would show me. (AN, p. 53)

If these characters grouped around Isabel in the novel all exist to answer James's "primary question" as to what Isabel will "do," then they clearly help define not simply the range of her field of action but also, and more importantly, its limits. Three of these characters function as Isabel's suitors; two are interested in her marrying their particular candidates; four have participated in marriages conspicuously unsuccessful. In short, the characters who constitute Isabel's milieu and who help determine the answer to the question "Well, what will she do?" would seem to point to the idea that the real question of the novel is "whom will she marry?"[8]

A just appreciation of the intensity with which this question informs the *Portrait* and establishes marriage as the sole condition of existence for a woman is crucial to any accurate appraisal of Isabel's character and behavior in the novel.[9] At the same time, however, the novel itself admits of no such simple response as this statement might suggest, for Isabel's growth in the course of the novel is made possible precisely by her own grim marriage. Isabel may represent the typical condition of women in the nineteenth century, and her career may chart the stultifying characteristics of that condition— and in this sense the *Portrait* does indeed reflect some of James's most searching criticism of the social conditions of his time. But the novel also reflects some of James's own abiding beliefs, most notably his belief in the supreme value of personal relationships, a belief underlying virtually all of his fiction.[10] As he was to tell the American women graduating from Bryn Mawr in 1905, "all life comes back to the question of our relations with each other."[11]

Despite James's confidence in the immense importance of personal relationships, however, he himself seemed to entertain very ambivalent feelings about the most intimate kind of personal relationship—the kind that in some senses represents the subject of the *Portrait*—marriage. James himself, of course, never married. After the death of his cousin Minny Temple, moreover, he rejoiced that Minny had "gone where there is neither marrying nor giving in marriage! no illusion and no disillusion—no sleepless nights and no ebbing strength."[12] "Marrying" and "giving in marriage," "illusion" and "disillusion" strike, of course, some of the major chords of the *Portrait*, whose heroine, as we have noted, is generally acknowledged to be based at least in part on Minny Temple.[13] Given the wretchedness informing most of the marriages in the novel, James might indeed find relief in Minny's removal from such a world. But other evidence from his letters suggests, paradoxically, that James regarded marriage as something good, though not for himself. To his brother William, for example, James wrote: "I believe almost as much in matrimony for most other people as I believe in it little for myself."[14] And, in 1881 when the *Portrait* was being published, he wrote to Grace Norton: "I am unlikely ever to marry. . . .One's attitude toward marriage is a part—the most characteristic part, doubtless—of one's general attitude toward life. . . . if I were to marry I should be guilty in my own eyes of inconsistency—I should pretend to think just a little better of life than I really do."[15]

The ambivalence suggested by these comments finds its way into the *Portrait*, where marriage seems to operate on two different levels: on the level of the universal, James treats marriage almost as a metaphor for a commitment to life itself (just as his letter to Grace Norton seems to do);[16] on the level of the particular, however, he boldly delineates the specific horrors that arise from the various marriages in the novel.[17] James's heroine has sometimes been judged harshly for her failure to resolve the opposition that inevitably arises from any confrontation of the universal and the particular, but Isabel Archer cannot resolve the opposition because it inheres in James's own inconsistent attitudes and beliefs. James resolved it for himself, surely, by virtue of his being a man and of his commitment to art; as Quentin Anderson has observed, the ending of the *Portrait,* which frequently leaves readers extremely dissatisfied, may in fact have resulted from James's discovery that it was "impossible to make Isabel Archer over into a man and launch her on the career of an artist."[18] That strong sense of identification which James felt with his American girls thus creates problems for him in this novel, for Isabel's tragedy cannot be averted—as perhaps James's own was—by a commitment to art. For her, as for most women of the nineteenth century, such an escape from marriage was impossible.

III

When Isabel Archer informs her cousin that she has decided to marry Gilbert Osmond, Ralph Touchett attempts to dissuade her by appealing to her love of freedom:

> "You were the last person I expected to see caught."
> "I don't know why you call it caught."
> "Because you're going to be put into a cage."
> "If I like my cage, that needn't trouble you," she
> answered. (IV, 65)

Though Isabel has at this moment no understanding of how little to her liking will be the particular cage that marriage to Osmond will provide her, she registers no surprise or outrage at Ralph's prediction that she is "to be put into a cage." On the contrary, Isabel throughout the novel has viewed marriage of any sort as a cage that would limit her freedom. For example, when Lord Warburton proposes to her we are told that "though she was lost in admiration of her opportunity she managed to move back into the deepest shade of it, even as some wild, caught creature in a vast cage" (III, 152-53). And, of course, her primary experience of her American suitor, Caspar Goodwood, is that "he seemed to deprive her of the sense of freedom" (III, 162). Isabel's realization—and it is an accurate one in 1870—that in marrying she would surrender the freedom she so prizes represents, in fact, her primary motivation in rejecting the proposals of both Lord Warburton and Caspar Goodwood. The reader, like Ralph Touchett in the conversation above, might well wonder, from Isabel's apparent understanding that her marriage to Gilbert Osmond will put her into a cage, what has become of her love of freedom. Isabel seems to have decided that freedom is no longer so appealing an ideal; she articulates such an idea when she says to Ralph that life no longer seems to her "such an inviting expanse" (IV, 65). There are, however, several forces at work in Isabel's decision to marry Osmond which her claim that "one must choose a corner and cultivate that" (IV, 65) does not really acknowledge. One of these is the ambiguous force exerted on her by her fortune, and the other is the force of her absolute conviction, a conviction not acknowledged in this conversation with Ralph, that she can marry Osmond and yet maintain her freedom as well.

The fortune that Ralph arranges for Isabel, to enable her to "meet the requirements" of her imagination, proves a curse to her not simply because it makes her a victim of the fortune-hunting Madame Merle and Gilbert Osmond but also because it adversely affects her conception of her own identity. Isabel's conception of her identity contributes to her early determination to remain single. She most forcefully asserts that determination in the interview in London with Caspar Goodwood that culminates in her "banishment" of Caspar for two years. To buttress his argument that Isabel should marry him, Caspar cleverly reminds her of those social realities that prevent an unmarried woman from being free:

> "An unmarried woman—a girl of your age—isn't independent. There are all sorts of things she can't do. She's hampered at every step."

"That's as she looks at the question," Isabel answered
with much spirit. "I'm not in my first youth—I can do
what I choose—I belong quite to the independent class.
I've neither father nor mother; I'm poor and of a serious
disposition; I'm not pretty. I therefore am not bound to
be timid and conventional; indeed I can't afford such
luxuries." (III, 228)

Isabel's final words in this passage ironically foreshadow the
"conventional" life that her fortune, placed in the hands of
Gilbert Osmond, enables her to "afford." More significant,
however, is her conviction that her lack of social and financial
status actually guarantees her freedom. Having nothing—no
parents, no social position, and no money—allows her, as she
sees it, at least to have herself and her liberty. In the sense that
she is not a valuable article in the marketplace of prospective
wives, Isabel's statement does reflect certain social realities,[19]
and thus to some extent justifies her confidence when she tells
Caspar, at the end of their conversation, to "remember too that
I shall not be an easy victim!" (III, 230).

But by the time Isabel next meets Caspar Goodwood, in
Florence on the eve of her marriage to Gilbert Osmond, she
has demonstrated to the reader just how easy a victim she is.
Her possession of an attractive fortune and those aspects of her
own character that make Gilbert Osmond appealing to her
contribute, of course, to this victimization. Equally important,
however, are her attitude toward the fortune her uncle leaves
her and the consequent change in her it creates.[20] For the
freedom she felt she possessed when she possessed nothing else
seems to disappear with her acquisition of a large fortune.

"Solemn" and "stupefied" by Mr. Touchett's bequest to her,
Isabel initially finds herself oppressed by the "new
consciousness" the inheritance brings her (III, 299, 300, 301).
The narrator goes on to comment that

> this failure to rise to immediate joy was indeed but brief;
> the girl presently made up her mind that to be rich was a
> virtue because it was to be able to *do*, and that to do could
> only be sweet. It was the graceful contrary of the stupid
> side of weakness—especially the feminine variety. To be
> weak was, for a delicate young person, rather graceful,

but, after all, as Isabel said to herself, there was a larger
grace than that. . . . The acquisition of power made her
serious; she scrutinised her power with a kind of tender
ferocity, but was not eager to exercise it. (III, 301)

As this passage suggests, the oppression Isabel experiences
from her newly acquired wealth stems from her belief that it
necessitates action, it makes her "able to *do*." And though she
is "not eager to exercise" the power her wealth brings her, she
feels here—and the feeling only increases as the novel moves
forward—that at some point this power must be exercised. The
necessity to rationalize her wealth as something good ("but,
after all, as Isabel said to herself") seems to spring from
Isabel's uncomfortable awareness of a transformation of her
identity; her fortune rids her of a certain weakness—"the
feminine variety" of weakness. But if it thereby confers on her
a kind of masculine power, it finds her pitifully unprepared to
know how to accept such power or how to integrate it
successfully with her own sense of her feminine identity.

This fairy-tale transformation from rags to riches, from
powerlessness to at least one kind of powerfulness,
distinguishes Isabel from some of James's earlier American
girls and from both of the later American girls. Milly Theale
and Maggie Verver are from the outset inordinately wealthy,
and their wealth operates, unlike Isabel's, as an integral aspect
of their identities. James's attitude toward wealth also seems
different from his attitude toward it here in the *Portrait*.[21]
Money in the *Portrait* is somewhat similar to money in *The
American* and in *The American Scene*, where, as we have seen,
it functions as a powerful symbol of masculinity. Thus, unlike
Milly and Maggie, Isabel experiences her fortune as a threat to
her sense of her essential femininity; her fortune is something
foreign to her, something apart from her conception of her
identity.

This fact helps explain her apparent change in attitude
toward the ideal of freedom, when she says to Ralph, "a large
fortune means freedom, and I'm afraid of that. It's such a fine
thing, and one should make such a good use of it. If one
shouldn't one would be ashamed. And one must keep
thinking; it's a constant effort. I'm not sure it's not a greater

happiness to be powerless" (III, 320). Isabel's fear of freedom as she expresses it here would seem to reveal certain inconsistencies in her character, or a change in her character, since freedom has been, to this point in the novel, her most cherished ideal. In fact, however, her fortune has brought her a totally new kind of freedom, which is related to action and which she has no inkling of how to exercise; the dissociation from her fortune which she seems to feel is here suggested by her repetition of the third person pronoun. For the kind of freedom Isabel has previously desired and experienced may be termed negative; it has been conceived and exercised by Isabel as the power to avoid restraints and limitations, most importantly the restraints and limitations that would ensue from marriage. Freedom for Isabel has meant the power to say "no" to her suitors. The fact that this freedom has really been another of Isabel's many illusions, that, as Freud and subsequent thinkers make clear, no self is ever free in the way Isabel has yearned to be, need not trouble us here. Isabel's early refusal to define herself in the way ordinarily open to women—that is, through marriage—has been one of her most distinguishing characteristics, and certainly has influenced Ralph Touchett's decision to provide her a fortune. But Isabel herself has not been altogether confident of her access even to this freedom, as evidenced by her repeated feelings of guilt for having rejected Caspar Goodwood and by her uncertainty and anxiety about Lord Warburton's respecting her answer of "no" to his proposal.

If Isabel has uncertainty about her ability to exercise this negative freedom, she is overwhelmed by the new freedom her inheritance seems to bring her. For her fortune, at least as she views it, introduces her to a new kind of freedom, a positive freedom, a freedom to *do*. Mr. Touchett's legacy bestows on Isabel a power and even a necessity to act; she feels that she would be "ashamed" if she did not make "a good use of it." Yet Isabel, like most of her real-life counterparts, has no notion of what "good use" she should make of her fortune. The world of action is a man's world for which Isabel has never been prepared and into which, despite her fortune, she would not really be allowed to enter; this fact becomes painfully obvious to her after her marriage: "she gave an envious thought to the happier lot of men, who are always free to plunge into the healing waters of action" (IV, 130). This "happier lot of men" is denied Isabel in part because she is a woman and in part because she is, as Baym observes, "unfitted by her protected and insulated background, by her lack of training and discipline, and by a 'romantic' temperament encouraged by her circumstances."[22]

Although Isabel eventually achieves a less troubled consciousness about her fortune, and although she contemplates "the fine things to be done by a rich, independent, generous girl" (III, 321), the only context for action which her background, experience, and gender (the first two determined, to no small extent, by the last) provide her is that of marriage; if she can learn to wield the power her fortune has given her, it will be in that arena only that she will be able to do so. Thus, it is hardly surprising that her fortune exerts a strong force on her during Gilbert Osmond's courtship of her. Although aspects of Isabel's character may contribute to her decision to marry Osmond, the fact of her fortune, juxtaposed to the fact of his poverty, assumes crucial importance. Because her fortune reverses the roles ordinarily associated with the man and the woman in a courtship, it creates guilt in Isabel and at the same time makes Osmond seem a less threatening suitor than Caspar Goodwood and Lord Warburton have been.

Isabel's feelings of guilt about her fortune surface most visibly in the scene in her hotel room in Rome which climaxes with Osmond's declaration of his love for her. Telling him of her plans to travel, to see the world, Isabel expresses discomfort that she should have the means to travel while he does not, especially since he seems so much worthier than she: "It wouldn't be remarkable if you did think it ridiculous that I should have the means to travel when you've not; for you know everything, and I know nothing" (IV, 15). Isabel's discomfort seems to originate in her sense that her fortune has given her a kind of masculine power and that this is somehow wrong; when she says to Osmond that "you see my ignorance, my blunders, the way I wander about as if the world belonged to me, simply because—because it has been put into my power to do so. You don't think a woman ought to do that" (IV, 14), she reveals the extent to which she has internalized the masculine assumptions about femininity that underlie the nineteenth-century world she inhabits. Osmond's poverty intensifies the initial threat posed by her fortune to her femininity. Her wealth and the unnatural power she thinks it brings give her the kind of masculine opportunities that Osmond's relative poverty makes inaccessible to him. Thus, their socially defined sexual roles have been reversed, which produces both guilt and uncertainty in Isabel.[23] As she reflects later, after her marriage has become a kind of horror, she had felt that marrying Osmond would "rub off a certain grossness attaching to the good luck of an unexpected inheritance. There had been nothing very delicate in inheriting seventy thousand pounds" (IV, 193). Her language here—"grossness," "delicate"—reinforces this idea that her fortune has somehow tainted her femininity.

Yet, as Isabel later reflects, the guilt her fortune produces, the necessity to act that it creates, and her consequent "desire to transfer the weight of it to some other conscience" have featured as only "half the story" that explains her marriage (IV, 193). For the reversal of sexual roles that contributes to her guilt also removes the fear she had experienced with her other suitors, allowing her finally to cross that "dusky, uncertain tract" of marriage (IV, 22). Her fortune gives her, she believes, a masculine power that enables her to "surrender to him with a kind of humility," to "marry him with a kind of pride," because "she was not only taking, she was giving" (IV, 82). Isabel's ability to be a contributor in a marriage to Osmond is, of course, exactly what she would conspicuously have lacked in a marriage to either Goodwood or Warburton. Just as she would have been the "property" of her other suitors, had she married them, so she feels that Osmond, "the finest—in the sense of being the subtlest—manly organism she had ever known had become her property" (IV, 194). Even her love for Osmond seems to have been created by her mistaken conviction that she, rather than he, would be the agent of power in their marriage, as the sequence of clauses in this sentence suggests: "She would launch his boat for him; she would be his providence; it would be a good thing to love him" (IV, 192).[24] Isabel's desire to give and to serve seems to be rooted in her need for power, an idea that has led some critics to judge her harshly.[25] Clearly, however, this need for power has its roots not in egoism but rather in Isabel's need to insure that her own self is not engulfed by another's, as it would have been in a marriage to either Goodwood or Warburton. If the social world depicted in the *Portrait* justifies Isabel's desire for power, the events of the novel testify that Isabel's belief that she could actually possess or exercise such power in a marriage with Osmond—or any man—is erroneous, a delusion. She has simply mistaken one usual symbol of the power structure of marriage—money—for the power itself.

This mistake is the most tragic of Isabel's career. The very real power embodied in Caspar Goodwood and Lord Warburton is what has threatened to "deprive" Isabel of her freedom, that is, of her integrity of self. Thus, she reasons, a marriage in which she has the power (symbolized by her fortune) would insure her continued freedom. By such fatal logic Isabel enters the "cage" of marriage to Osmond. The momentary, partial reversal of sexual roles effected by her fortune deludes Isabel into believing that her financial power can constitute a continuous, real power that will allow her to marry and maintain her freedom as well. Her realization of the mutual exclusivity of marriage and freedom becomes the bitterest revelation of all: "she had suddenly found the infinite vista of a multiplied life to be a dark, narrow alley with a dead wall at the end" (IV, 189).

The stultifying qualities in Isabel's marriage to Osmond exaggerate and distort, but nevertheless reflect, the general limitations inhering in the world presented in the novel; Isabel eventually comes to recognize how little she has understood the nature of the world she inhabits. Her desire to find fulfillment through a personal relationship is, the narrator tells us early in the novel, paramount: "Deep in her soul—it was the deepest thing there—lay a belief that if a certain light should dawn she could give herself completely" (III, 71-72). This idea, however, is "too formidable to be attractive" (III, 72), and what seems to make it formidable is her realization that "to give herself completely" would be to revoke her own freedom and integrity.[26] The attractiveness of a man like Gilbert Osmond resides in his not resembling at all the masculine figures of power and energy she has previously known, and this fact, combined with his poverty and the power she believes her fortune will give her, leads Isabel to think she can have both the fulfillment and enrichment of a personal, intimate relationship and her freedom as well.

Yet Isabel's marriage provides neither freedom nor fulfillment in a personal relationship; it becomes, on the contrary, "the house of darkness, the house of dumbness, the house of suffocation" (IV, 196) in which husband and wife share no intimacy at all. Isabel's recognition of this reality forces upon her the question that is the concern of the last third of the novel: "What was coming? What was before them? That was her constant question. What would he do—what ought *she* to do? When a man hated his wife what did it lead to?" (IV, 202). What Isabel's friends—Henrietta Stackpole, Ralph Touchett, Caspar Goodwood—and many readers of the novel want it to lead to is divorce or separation. Isabel's return to Osmond at the end of the novel has thus become a focal point of critical discussions of the *Portrait*. The fact that the other characters in the novel encourage Isabel to leave Osmond makes it difficult to explain her refusal to do so entirely in terms of the fact that in the 1870s divorce was not really an option for a woman. Other interpretations of Isabel's return to Osmond are even less satisfactory—for example, that she prefers the sterile Osmond to the virile Goodwood, or that she herself has become enslaved by empty conventions and meaningless forms.

Isabel's return to Osmond must be understood as her own conscious effort to view her life as meaningful. Although she has become aware, by the novel's end, of many of the ways in which she was earlier deluded, the mechanism that led to her youthful self-delusions is still functioning. She must somehow make meaningful the suffering she experiences, and the final chapters of the novel dramatize her creation of constructs that will render her experiences rational and valuable. Although

Isabel's marriage brings her pain and unhappiness, she will not end it or flee from it because she regards it, as she must, as a commitment of the highest sort: "the most serious act—the single sacred act—of her life" (IV, 246). She can only regard it, therefore, as the "scene of the rest of my life" (IV, 398).

The final chapters of the *Portrait* attest that Isabel's marriage and, more important, her continuation in it, do in fact, in her mind, constitute her commitment to life itself. She reflects, for example, during her journey from Rome to Gardencourt to visit the dying Ralph in defiance of her husband's wishes, that "she envied Ralph his dying, for if one were thinking of rest that was the most perfect of all. To cease utterly, to give it all up and not know anything more—this idea was as sweet as the vision of a cool bath in a marble tank, in a darkened chamber, in a hot land" (IV, 391). Particularly significant in this passage is the phrase "and not know anything more," for Isabel believes that her willingness to *know*, to confront with a full consciousness the horrid realities of her marriage—Osmond's feelings toward her and motives for marrying her, Madame Merle's betrayal, her own participation in creating it—is what makes her life defensible. For a similar reason, Isabel, unlike Madame de Mauves, does not attempt to anesthetize herself to the suffering knowledge brings; on the contrary, the narrator observes that "suffering, with Isabel, was an active condition; it was not a chill, a stupor, a despair; it was a passion of thought, of speculation, of response to every pressure" (IV, 189). Thus, what Isabel finds attractive in death is the cessation of knowing and of the pain which knowledge often brings. But though death momentarily appeals to her, she recognizes that "this privilege was evidently to be denied her. Deep in her soul—deeper than any appetite for renunciation—was the sense that life would be her business for a long time to come" (IV, 392). The resistance to knowledge and consequent suffering demonstrated by some of James's other American girls is thus overcome by Isabel Archer.

Her commitment to life, then, means a commitment to a life of consciousness, to keeping her eyes steadily open to the knowledge and truth of her life (and she believes she always sees that knowledge and truth), and thereby involves a consequent acceptance of the suffering unavoidably accompanying this knowledge.[27] A lack of this sort of commitment to life, by contrast, has made Isabel's aunt, Mrs. Touchett, really an instance of death-in-life; meeting her aunt in Gardencourt when Ralph is dying, Isabel finds herself wondering whether Mrs. Touchett would not "have found it a blessing to-day to be able to feel a defeat, a mistake, even a shame or two. She wondered if she [Mrs. Touchett] were not even missing those enrichments of consciousness and privately trying—reaching out for some aftertaste of life, dregs of the banquet" (IV, 406). "Enrichments of consciousness" can be acquired, clearly, only through the experience of "a defeat," or "a mistake," or "a shame or two"—for these constitute the "banquet" of life. This interpretation is the central myth which Isabel creates in order to make her own life bearable.

The greatest testimony to Isabel's secure possession of such "enrichments of consciousness" and to her sense of her growth since the outset of her career is, of course, her vision of the ghost at Gardencourt on the morning Ralph dies. Early in her career, when she first arrived at Gardencourt, Isabel had asked Ralph to show her the ghost:

> Ralph shook his head sadly. "I might show it to you, but you'd never see it. The privilege isn't given to everyone; it's not enviable. It has never been seen by a young, happy, innocent person like you. You must have suffered first, have suffered greatly, have gained some miserable knowledge. In that way your eyes are opened to it. I saw it long ago," said Ralph.
> "I told you just now I'm very fond of knowledge," Isabel answered.
> "Yes, of happy knowledge—of pleasant knowledge. But you haven't suffered, and you're not made to suffer. I hope you'll never see the ghost." (III, 64)

As Isabel's marriage to Osmond has seemed to make clear to her, gaining the "miserable knowledge" and experiencing the suffering necessary to open her eyes to the ghost entail an enormously high price. Though Isabel insists in this early conversation that "it's not absolutely necessary to suffer; we were not made for that" (III, 65), she comes to believe, by the end of the novel, that suffering is indeed "necessary," that we are indeed "made for that" if we wish to participate in the "banquet" of life. Isabel's willingness to accept this suffering as a "necessary condition" for a life of consciousness empowers her finally to see the ghost: "He had told her, the first evening she ever spent at Gardencourt, that if she should live to suffer enough she might some day see the ghost with which the old house was duly provided. She apparently had fulfilled the necessary condition; for the next morning, in the cold, faint dawn, she knew that a spirit was standing by her bed" (IV, 418).

Banta has argued that Isabel has been able "to gain the privileged pain of facing the ghost of Gardencourt" only because she has been willing to live "into the experience whose meaning Ralph Touchett understands from the first"—the experience, that is, of good and evil.[28] One might add, however, that Isabel's seeing of the ghost, a goal defined by Ralph Touchett, is a necessary experience if her adventures in Europe are not to have meant nothing. If her marriage to Gilbert Osmond is to be made a truly "sacred act," then the suffering it has brought must be made meaningful and good. Isabel's encounter with Gardencourt's ghost creates that meaning and insures that good. It represents her acceptance of Ralph's vision of the world; she has come to believe, like Ralph, that suffering is the necessary condition of being fully human. It is, of course, painfully ironic to the reader that such convictions have led the real Isabels of the world to embrace unrewarding and unfulfilling ways of life. It is also perhaps inevitable that Isabel, who prides herself on her willingness to confront the truth, represses the truth that Ralph has been her ultimate betrayer, manipulating her life in ways worthy of Osmond, and opts instead to accept as worthy Ralph's ethic of suffering.[29]

Isabel's return to her marriage with Osmond thus reflects her acceptance of what she believes the conditions of life to be. She believes that a permanent retreat or escape from Osmond would constitute a desire to escape from the realities of life itself. The mechanism that allows her to see the ghost thus also determines the way she interprets Caspar Goodwood's offer to "save" her from her marriage. In words that echo her own in the early stages of her career, he says to her, "We can do absolutely as we please. Were we born to rot in our misery? . . . If you'll only trust me, how little you will be disappointed! The world's all before us—and the world's very big" (IV, 435). Caspar's offer represents a temptation for Isabel to escape from and deny what she has come to define as life itself, as is made clear by her response to it; the narrator comments: "I know not whether she believed everything he said; but she believed just then that to let him take her in his arms would be *the next best thing to her dying*" (IV, 435; my emphasis). As we have seen, though Isabel has momentarily "envied Ralph his dying," she has felt "deep in her soul" that "life would be her business for a long time to come." And as we have also seen, Isabel has come to equate life with suffering, in an attempt to make her past and present life somehow meaningful. Thus, when she runs from Goodwood's embrace she does so because she believes that however attractive Goodwood's offer may be, its appeal resembles the appeal of death—it is, in fact, in her mind the "next best thing" to death. Her commitment is to life, and her life exists where she has created it, in her marriage to Gilbert Osmond.

IV

If Isabel Archer's return to Gilbert Osmond represents for many readers the most unsettling and unsatisfying gesture in the novel, it can nevertheless be largely explained in terms of James's deliberate effort to work in the *Portrait* within the confines of realism. As a character who reflects the actual possibilities—including psychological possibilities—open to a woman of the 1870s, Isabel must inevitably, perhaps, decide to celebrate suffering and return to her marriage. Like most actual unions of the nineteenth century, Isabel's marriage is confining; like most actual women of her day, Isabel must define herself in terms of her marriage; and like most women of her day caught in such marriages, she has open to her only the "freedom" of deciding to view that marriage as a commitment to life.

Preoccupied, as we have seen, from the outset of his career with the feminine American sensibility, James for the first time in the *Portrait* attempts a fully rounded, complex portrayal of that sensibility. Yet by placing his heroine in a socially realistic novel, he discovered the limitations of the figure when she was conceived of and presented within the bounds of realism. At best the American girl treated in realistic fiction can have but a muted triumph because the powers of her femininity and her consciousness are inevitably limited by the world the fiction forces her to inhabit. For James forcefully demonstrates that Isabel is controlled by the male world in ways far more insidious than she herself is aware. He shows us that behind the "cage" of Isabel's marriage is the cage of her own mind, for she has unconsciously internalized those values of the male world which function to keep her an imprisoned and unquestioning victim. Gilbert Osmond will need no external restraints on a wife who believes that the strength of her commitment to life is attested by the intensity of her suffering.

Thus, although she is not one of the many pathetic women of the nineteenth century who, like James's sister Alice, languished from psychosomatic illnesses, Isabel Archer does succumb in her own way to the nineteenth-century male's restrictions upon woman. And just as James noted that his sister Alice's tragic illness was "in a manner the only solution for her of the practical problem of life,"[30] so he shows us that Isabel's acceptance of a life of suffering is her own "solution" to the problem of her life. We cannot, certainly, condemn her, for however disturbing a character she is, her realistic dimensions make her James's most humanly appealing American girl.[31] The psychologically crippling conditions of the realistic fictional world she inhabits necessitate the kind of defensive illusions she creates.

5

"Heiress of All the Ages" and Bankruptcy of Self: *The Wings of the Dove*

I had from far back mentally projected a certain sort of young American as more the "heir of all the ages" than any other young person whatever . . . so that here was a chance to confer on some such figure a supremely touching value. To be the heir of all the ages only to know yourself, as that consciousness should deepen, balked of your inheritance, would be to play the part, it struck me, or at least to arrive at the type, in the light on the whole the most becoming.

—Preface, The Wings of the Dove

I

With the publication of *The Wings of the Dove* in 1902, James announced in effect his embarkation on a new way of writing the novel, his "third method" as his brother William called it,[1] a method made possible in part by his decision no longer to plan his novels according to the needs of serial publication— that avenue of publication having become increasingly shut off to him. But though *The Wings of the Dove* reflects the "Late Style" of James, in it he returned to that on which his career had first been established, the international theme, and he employed once again the figure of the American girl to work out that theme for him. Moreover, his new style freed him from the restraints imposed by the realistic methods of *The Portrait of a Lady* and created for him the possibility of exploring fully the psychology of the American girl. Thus, though the style of *The Wings of the Dove* was new, the subject of the novel represented for James, as he says in the Preface to the New York Edition, "a very old—if I shouldn't perhaps rather say a very young—motive; I can scarce remember the time when the situation on which this long-drawn fiction mainly rests was not vividly present to me" *(AN,* p. 288). Although this novel does not, like *The Portrait of a Lady,* center itself on the American girl Milly Theale, in James's mind her situation nevertheless forms the central idea of the novel: "The idea, reduced to its essence, is that of a young person conscious of a great capacity for life, but early stricken and doomed, condemned to die under short respite, while also enamoured of the world" *(AN,* p. 288).

James's sense that this doomed young person could only have been an American woman *(AN,* pp. 288, 292) establishes a crucial new base in his imaginative treatment of the figure of the American girl. For if Milly Theale is condemned to death by a fatal illness, and if, as James says in the Preface, that condition constituted "the most becoming" way in which to present his American heiress of all the ages, then clearly her fatal illness might be viewed as a symbol or metaphor for an inner deficiency created by her situation as an American woman. James's ambiguous treatment of Milly Theale's illness in the novel gives credence to this idea: Milly's illness remains mysteriously unnamed, her eminent physician Sir Luke Strett suggests that love may be a cure for it, and she dies by an act of apparent volition—she "turns her face to the wall." Thus, although the novel's very plot can be enacted only by virtue of the other characters' conviction that Milly does suffer from a fatal illness, equal importance is placed, in part through the mysterious and ambiguous treatment of her disease, on the spiritual deficiency that unfits Milly for life. Importantly, both in the novel and in the Preface to it, James suggests that Milly's illness is rooted in some way in her cultural identity; she is "the last fine flower. . .of an 'old' New York stem" (*AN*, p. 292), and she has lost, in her short life, all her family through "a high extravagance of speculation and dissipation" (XIX, 174). By thus dooming his heroine to a physical illness somehow engendered by her cultural identity, James asserts the crucial role this identity plays in making the American girl "but the sport of fate" (*AS*, p. 348). Moreover, because Milly's psychology functions as an analogue of her physical illness,[2] the novel demonstrates just how crippling the American girl's psychology can be. For it is not simply Milly Theale's physical malady that makes her a ready victim of Lancaster Gate and its milieu; more importantly, her own character and personality, of which her illness is both a result and a symbol, prevent her coming to terms with life.

Milly's psychological deficiencies have not, however, received the kind of critical attention that has been lavished on the similar deficiencies of her earlier counterpart, Isabel Archer, a fact that may be attributed to several causes. First, there is the undeniable effect of Milly's goodness and charity upon Merton Densher; coupled with the Biblical source of the novel's title,[3] this often invites religious interpretations of Milly's character itself.[4] Second, James's method of using multiple points of view in the novel and of centering only a minor portion of the novel on Milly's consciousness makes her character less accessible to the reader than is, for example, Isabel Archer's in *The Portrait of a Lady*. James makes clear, moreover, in an authorial intrusion in the Third Book of the novel, his reluctance to present Milly directly: "She worked—and seemingly quite without design—upon the sympathy, the curiosity, the fancy of her associates, and we shall really ourselves scarce otherwise come closer to her than by feeling their impression and sharing, if need be, their confusion" (XIX, 116). Finally, the fact that James intended *The Wings of the Dove* to be a tribute to the memory of his beloved cousin Minny Temple has tended to make readers reluctant to bring to Milly Theale's character the kind of scrutiny ordinarily accorded James's heroines, as it is perhaps responsible for James's decision to present this heroine so indirectly. These aspects of James's presentation of Milly Theale should not and cannot be dismissed. At the same time, however, a close analysis of the text reveals that Milly is doomed as much by her own psychology as by her illness; furthermore, this psychology which makes her unable to cope with life and yet reflects a spiritual purity that has redemptive effects on others accurately points to James's ambiguous feelings about Minny Temple, whose ghost, as he says in *Notes of a Son and Brother*, he had sought "to lay by wrapping it, a particular occasion aiding, in the beauty and dignity of art."[5]

"Laying the ghost" of Minny Temple figured for James as an effort to understand the riddle which her life had always seemed to him to represent. Though we have briefly noted James's ambivalence toward Minny Temple, it merits our renewed attention because of the especially close ties of Minny to Milly Theale. As James said in a letter to Grace Norton, Minny's "life was a strenuous, almost passionate *question*, which my mind, at least, lacked the energy to offer the elements of an answer for."[6] The question she posed perhaps grew out of the fact that she had "at once such noble flights and such touchingly discouraged drops."[7] On the one hand, James saw her as "the supreme case of a taste for life as life, as personal living";[8] on the other hand, the very intensity of this "taste for life as life" seemed paradoxically to alienate her from "a world to which she was essentially hostile."[9] "A plant of pure American growth," Minny represented to James both "her own sex ... but even more *Youth*,"[10] just as she embodied for him that rare moral spontaneity that he made so salient a characteristic of his fictional American girls. Though Minny "would have given anything to live,"[11] James felt that if she *had* lived, "poor narrow life—[would have] contained no place for her."[12] The delicate ambivalence that marks all of James's comments about Minny Temple is perhaps best reflected in a letter he wrote to William shortly after Minny's death on March 8, 1870:

> Her character may be almost literally said to have been without practical application to life. . . . She was at any rate the helpless victim and toy of her own intelligence— so that there is positive relief in thinking of her being removed from her own heroic treatment and placed in kinder hands. . . . She was restless ... she was helpless ... she was unpractical. . . . Her happiness like her unhappiness remained wholly incomplete. But what strikes me above all is how great and rare a benefit her life has been to those with whom she was associated. I feel as if a very fair portion of my sense of the reach and quality and capacity of human nature rested upon my experience of her character: certainly a large portion of my admiration of it.[13]

Minny Temple's thirst for life, her "sense for verity of character and play of life in others,"[14] her sensitivity, and her responsiveness made her, for James, at once the most wonderful creature he was ever to know and yet the least equipped for life in this world. Though James never fully explored, at least in print, the ways in which Minny's very virtues made her a victim, nor the elements of her psychology that, had she lived, would have made her future life "a sadly insoluble problem,"[15] he may be said to have done so in his commemorative novel, *The Wings of the Dove*. Just as Minny Temple seemed to James to have died "from having served her purpose" of bringing strength and hope to him,[16] so her fictional sister, Milly Theale, brings through her death a new kind of consciousness to Merton Densher. But just as James could distinguish the effect of Minny's death on him from those aspects of her personality that would have created difficulties for her had she lived, so too does he distinguish in his portrait of Milly Theale between her effect on those around her and those elements of her character that make life "a sadly insoluble problem" for her. In this way, then, Milly Theale represents the most virtuous and beatific and yet also the most helpless and deficient of all his American girls. Although my focus in the following pages will be on the latter qualities, James's own presentation clearly incorporates the former as well.

II

In the Preface to *The Wings of the Dove* James observes of his heroine that "a young person so devoted and exposed, a creature with her security hanging so by a hair, couldn't but fall somehow into some abysmal trap" *(AN,* p. 293), and the plot of the novel dramatizes the "abysmal trap" into which Milly Theale does fall—the materialistic machinations of Kate Croy and Merton Densher in particular and of the milieu of Lancaster Gate in general. What James fails to clarify in the Preface is how and why Milly is "devoted and exposed," and what makes her a ready victim of "that hard English gang."[17] If Milly's physical illness does in fact symbolize an inner deficiency which unfits her for "the whole assault of life" then clearly that inner deficiency demands our attention. Though I do not wish to present a pathological case study of Milly Theale,[18] I do believe that an examination of the psychological dynamics governing her character is crucial. A close analysis of the novel suggests that Milly, like many of James's earlier American girls, experiences extreme difficulty in living within the subjective "I"; she is surrounded, moreover, by characters who seek to deny her such a status. These two forces seem to thrust her into a defensive isolation and her course in the novel moves consistently in the direction of greater and greater passivity—until, in fact, James completely removes her from the novel. Through her bequest to Merton Densher, she continues to exert an influence on the world, but she can do so only by dying. And that death is, though perhaps unconsciously, to some extent self-willed.

James first introduces Milly into the novel from the romantic perspective of her Bostonian companion, Susan Shepherd Stringham, who establishes the view of Milly, later adopted by others in the novel, as a princess who is "the potential heiress of all the ages" (XIX, 109). Although Susan Stringham's perceptions of Milly are colored and distorted by her own romantic proclivities and by her awe of the New York fortune which for her defines Milly Theale, her section of the novel (Book Third) nevertheless establishes the essential fragility of Milly and describes the tension that exists between her great fortune and her naive innocence. In terms very like those we have seen James use in his description of the American girl in *The American Scene (AS,* pp. 346-49), Susan reflects on the disparity between the possibilities which Milly's status affords her and her lack of any preparation that would allow her to realize those possibilities: "It was rich, romantic, abysmal, to have, as was evident, thousands and thousands a year, to have youth and intelligence and, if not beauty, at least in equal measure a high dim charming ambiguous oddity, which was even better, and then on top of all to enjoy boundless freedom, the freedom of the wind in the desert—it was unspeakably touching to be so equipped and yet to have been reduced by fortune to little humbleminded mistakes" (XIX, 110).

The "consenting bewilderment" to which Milly reduces Susan Stringham (XIX, 117) emerges again and again from Susan's attempts to understand this princess to whom she has attached herself. Overall, however, the keynote of her reflections is this sense that Milly's fortune and social status are not matched by a strong and self-confident personality. Like Isabel Archer in *The Portrait of a Lady,* Milly fatally lacks important knowledge and abilities; it is for these, perhaps, that she has come to Europe. The climax of Mrs. Stringham's reflections comes with Milly's first direct appearance in the novel—she is sitting alone, high on the edge of an Alpine cliff. Though this Alpine scene admits of various symbolic interpretations, its most immediate effect is to create in the reader an awareness of the solitariness and the precariousness of Milly Theale's life: "Mrs. Stringham stifled a cry in taking in what she believed to be the danger of such a perch for a mere maiden: her liability to slip, to slide, to leap, to be precipitated by a single false movement, by a turn of the head—how could one tell? into whatever was beneath" (XIX, 123). Milly's precarious perch suggests symbolically, as Matthiessen has said, "that the menace of death is always near";[19] but the language of the passage also implies that this menace may originate either in an external source—"her liability to slip, to slide . . . to be precipitated by a single false movement"—or in an internal compulsion "to leap" into the abyss. Important, too, is the idea that Milly's precariousness stems at least in part from her being a "mere maiden." Although Mrs. Stringham eventually decides that Milly "was not meditating a jump" (XIX, 124), through the language of the passage James has succeeded in establishing Milly's self-destructive potential. As Susan Stringham continues to reflect on what this image of Milly might mean, she describes what will become the true test to which the novel puts Milly:

> For she now saw that the great thing she had brought away was precisely a conviction that the future was not to exist for her princess in the form of any sharp or simple release from the human predicament. It wouldn't be for her a question of a flying leap and thereby of a quick escape. It would be a question of taking full in the face the whole assault of life, to the general muster of which indeed her face might have been directly presented as she sat there on the rock. (XIX, 125)

"The whole assault of life" proves to be what Milly attempts in the subsequent action of the novel to bear, but it is a rather short-lived attempt in part because life appears to her too complex and too painful. Ironic, also, is Mrs. Stringham's conviction here that Milly would not take "a flying leap" in order to effect "a quick escape" from life, since she does die only six months after this Alpine scene. Milly's mysterious illness, like Minny Temple's tuberculosis, fortuitously allows her "a quick escape" and thus prevents her from having to take "the whole assault of life."

London provides the scene of life for Milly, and it is a London of prey and predators, where nobody "does anything for nothing" (XIX, 160). Yet while Milly's goodness and her fortune make her an obvious victim for Maud Lowder and, eventually, Kate Croy, the primary threat that the milieu of Lancaster Gate poses is to her conception of her self. Milly's venture into the society of Lancaster Gate challenges her, perhaps for the first time, to wonder who or what she is. Throughout the novel the other characters project ready-made identities for Milly: she is Mrs. Stringham's princess, she is an American heiress of all the ages, she is an American girl. Initially, Milly herself rejects these simplistic and reductive identities and strives instead to live within a more complex subjectivity. This initial effort, however, is rather quickly overcome by Milly's inability to withstand the fear and the pain inevitably accompanying such an attempt. The primary agent effecting this reversal is Kate Croy, which may explain why James draws so many parallels in the novel between these two characters.[20] Kate can be seen to function for Milly as an alter ego or ego ideal: she is the person Milly would in some ways like to be but believes she cannot be, and she is both loved and hated by Milly.

Kate Croy is for Milly, from the outset of her stay in London, the most important aspect of the scene; and what Milly feels most acutely are the great differences between herself and Kate. For example, at the dinner given by Maud Lowder in honor of Milly and Mrs. Stringham, just a few days after their arrival in London, Milly wonders whether Lord Mark, who is seated next to her at dinner, might be able to tell her "why she was so different from the handsome girl [Kate Croy]—which she didn't know, being merely able to feel it; or at any rate might learn from him why the handsome girl was so different from her" (XIX, 153). By the end of this dinner, Milly has concluded that the striking difference between herself and "the handsome girl" resides in the fact that she is simple, while Kate is complex (XIX, 166), and her subsequent perceptions of Kate reflect her painful awareness of that difference. But clearly another important difference between Kate and Milly lies in Kate's greater physical beauty and in what Milly perceives to be her "talent for life." Early in their friendship, for example, before Milly has learned that Kate knows Merton Densher, she believes with certainty that Kate must have a male friend, "as yet unnamed . . . it being manifest that such a creature couldn't help having" (XIX, 173). Later, Milly concludes that Kate is "the least bit brutal" because she discovers that Kate finds Susan Stringham boring, and "it just faintly rankled in her that a person who was good enough and to spare for Milly Theale shouldn't be good enough for another girl" (XIX, 181).

Milly experiences her difference from Kate as an absence or lack of something within herself, a deficiency. Kate represents Milly's first experience of the Other, and, as Lacan makes clear, discovery of such a lack leads to a desire for unity, which in itself prompts a kind of identification with the Other. This desire for unity is, of course, ultimately a desire for death. Milly Theale's response to her encounter with the Other is most fully expressed after she realizes that Kate Croy knows Merton Densher. Milly's feelings about Merton Densher, and about Kate Croy in relation to Merton Densher, constitute, in fact, a major access in the novel to the psychological dynamics underlying her character.

Though her friends successfully deceive Milly about Kate's love for Densher, the mere fact that he loves Kate reinforces Milly's tendency to view herself in relation to Kate, and this view consistently creates in her feelings of helpless inadequacy. From the moment that she learns that Kate knows Densher, but has not confided this fact, Milly attaches undue and unnatural significance to what she considers Kate's deliberate "extrusion" of Densher from their conversations; at one point, Milly even irrationally reflects that she "could have made it out for herself that he had avoided the subject of Miss Croy [when he visited Milly in New York] and that Miss Croy was yet a subject it could never be natural to avoid" (XIX, 188). Though Milly's own infatuation with Densher, developed during his three visits to her in New York, contributes to her jealous anxiety that Kate and Densher might be attached to each other, it is primarily her sense of how much more attractive Kate is than she that constitutes the major threat:

"Twice over thus, for two or three hours together, Milly found herself seeing Kate, quite fixing her, in the light of the knowledge that it was a face on which Mr. Densher's eyes had more or less familiarly rested and which, by the same token, had looked, rather *more* beautifully than less, into his own" (XIX, 189-90).

These feelings of jealousy and feminine inadequacy triggered in Milly by Kate's acquaintance with Densher perhaps help explain her attempts to deceive herself about her own feelings for Densher. Her discussion with Mrs. Stringham about her conversation with Kate's sister, Mrs. Condrip, dramatically reveals such an attempt at self-deception. Milly evasively justifies to Mrs. Stringham her failure to reveal her own acquaintance with Densher to Mrs. Condrip, and her further failure to ask Mrs. Condrip whether Kate returns Densher's love. Not only is Milly reluctant to admit to herself her feelings for Densher, but she is also clearly frightened by them. When Mrs. Stringham reminds her that her acquaintance with Densher must eventually, on his return to London, be revealed to everyone, Milly responds:

> "I might get at him somehow beforehand," the girl suggested; "I might give him what they call here the 'tip'—that he's not to know me when we meet. Or, better still, I mightn't be here at all."
> "Do you want to run away from him?"
> It was, oddly enough, an idea Milly seemed half to accept. "I don't know *what* I want to run away from!"
> (XIX, 198-99)

Milly's acknowledged fear and her desire "to run away" prompt Mrs. Stringham, curiously, to remark with compassion that Milly is not "as sound and as strong as I insist on having you" (XIX, 199). To this Milly responds that even her *"most* 'beaux moments' aren't such as to qualify, so far as appearance goes, for anything gayer than a handsome cemetery," and that therefore "since I've lived all these years as if I were dead, I shall die, no doubt, as if I were alive" (XIX, 199).

The dramatic movement in this conversation from Milly's

fear of her feelings for Densher to her pronouncement on the appearance she will give when she dies reveals a much greater psychological complexity in James's treatment of her than critical discussions customarily acknowledge. The death-in-life which Milly presents as an accurate description of herself suggests how intensely and enormously vacant she has felt her life to be. Yet her feelings for Densher, which might make her life seem less empty, are apparently too threatening to entertain—let alone to act upon. She turns instead to death. And one attraction of death to her would seem to be the self-definition it can give her.

An object rather than a subject to other people, Milly becomes increasingly alienated from herself and begins to experience her own life as a drama unfolding before her. This detachment from life helps explain her attempt to view her grand afternoon at Matcham as "the pink dawn of an apotheosis" (XIX, 220) and her tearful identification with the lady of the Bronzino portrait, who "was a very great personage—only unaccompanied by a joy. And she was dead, dead, dead. Milly recognised her exactly in words that had nothing to do with her. 'I shall never be better than this'" (XIX, 221). This climaxing scene, which represents a turning point of sorts for Milly, has been the subject of much critical discussion and has often been viewed as a symbolic adumbration of the fact that Milly's "course is set towards death"[21] because her fatal illness is soon to overtake her. Yet, her fatal illness notwithstanding, Milly's virtual identification with the lady of the portrait and her concomitant belief that she "shall never be better than this" also reveal her increasing objectification of herself and her detachment of herself from life. The appeal which the portrait holds for Milly would seem to reside in its unity and fixedness. The lady of the portrait possesses a harmony not available to Milly, for it is the ultimate harmony of death,[22] and it is this harmony that Milly, from this point on in the novel, seems to desire.

As the Bronzino scene continues, moreover, Milly suddenly, intuitively, discovers the possible value of her physical illness. Minutes after she confronts the Bronzino, Kate Croy appears, and Milly immediately collapses in a moment of physical exhaustion. When Kate inquires if Milly is ill, Milly acknowledges to herself that she has in fact "sunk" into physical collapse in order to avoid the anxieties and fear engendered in her by Kate:

> Thus it was that, aloft there in the great gilded historic chamber and the presence of the pale personage on the wall, whose eyes all the while seemed engaged with her own, she found herself suddenly sunk in something quite intimate and humble and to which these grandeurs were strange enough witnesses. It had come up, in the form in which she had had to accept it, all suddenly, and nothing about it, at the same time, was more marked than that she had in a manner plunged into it to escape from something else. Something else, from her first vision of her friend's appearance three minutes before, had been present to her even through the call made by the others on her attention; something that was perversely *there*, she was more and more uncomfortably finding, at least for the first moments and by some spring of its own, with every renewal of their meeting. "Is it the way she looks to *him?*" she asked herself—the perversity being that she kept in remembrance that Kate was known to him. It wasn't a fault in Kate—nor in him assuredly; and she had a horror, being generous and tender, of treating either of them as if it had been. To Densher himself she couldn't make it up—he was too far away; but her secondary impulse was to make it up to Kate. (XIX, 225-26)

Milly's obsessive awareness of the fact that Kate knows Densher and her apparent feeling that Densher would find Kate, "the handsome girl," more attractive than herself arouses a turbulence within her. The contrast she senses between herself and Kate is particularly vivid to her here because she prefers to identify with the "pale personage" of the Bronzino rather than with the vibrant Kate. The reason for this preference would seem to be revealed in her thought that "it wasn't a fault in Kate—nor in him assuredly." Though for Kate and Densher to know each other is not "a fault," Milly apparently fears that she might treat them as if it were. The possibility of love and passion between Kate and Densher would seem, of course, to be the principal source of her anxiety. But what creates this chain of reactions is perhaps ultimately Milly's fear that she cannot be handsome and passionate like Kate, and this fear leads her to identify not with Kate but with the dead lady of the Bronzino portrait. Significantly, then, Milly realizes that she has taken refuge in her physical illness "to escape from something else," the something else figuring in one way or another as the stirring of passion within herself that has been triggered by Kate's presence and the memory of Densher associated with it.

This emotional process thus culminates in her decision to "make it up to Kate"; curiously, her way of "making it up" is to ask Kate to accompany her on the next day to Sir Luke Strett's—this favor, she feels, will demonstrate her loyalty to Kate. At the end of her conversation with Kate, Milly concludes that she has attained "just the point at which she had wished to arrive. She had wanted to prove to herself that she didn't horribly blame her friend for any reserve; and what better proof could there be than this quite special confidence? If she desired to show Kate that she really believed that Kate liked her, how could she show it more than by asking her help?" (XIX, 229). Milly "proves to herself" that she does not really resent Kate, and she "proves" to Kate that she believes in her friendship—the implicit equation here being that Kate can "prove" her liking for Milly only by confiding her acquaintance with Merton Densher. Milly's method of "making it up"—asking Kate to accompany her to Sir Luke Strett's—suggests, moreover, an unconscious desire to "get back" at Kate for her reserve. For in requesting that Kate go with her to the eminent physician's, Milly again seems to use, albeit unconsciously, her suspected illness to give her special status with Kate. Since Milly seems to believe that she cannot compete with Kate for Densher's love as a normal woman, then her way of "making it up" to Kate perhaps constitutes an effort to change the grounds of competition. Kate could not, certainly, compete with a dying girl. The simultaneous fear and inadequacy triggered in Milly by Kate, "the handsome girl" with her "talent for life," seems to drive Milly self-destructively to seek refuge in a fatal illness.

Milly's behavior in this scene with Kate also attests to her own desire to detach and isolate herself from others. Her action here, predicated on a desire to overlook any lapses in Kate's intimacy with her, effectually eliminates any further possibilities of intimacy. For she appeals to Kate's pity, despite her repeated attempts throughout the rest of the novel to deny others the privilege of pitying her. She presents herself as an object to Kate; she refuses to be a subject. After asking Kate to go with her to Sir Luke's, Milly actively solicits Kate's pity with such comments as, "I think I could die without its being noticed" (XIX, 228). And when Kate responds, as she can only do, with pity, Milly reflects that "exactly this—the handsome girl's compassionate manner, her friendly descent from her own strength—was what she had . . . foretold. She took Kate up as if positively for the deeper taste of it" (XIX, 228). Thus, Milly seems unconsciously to manipulate Kate—as she does the other characters—in order to forestall any possibility of genuine, or intimate, interaction. The fact that Kate herself requires little if any encouragement to regard Milly as an object need not concern us now. Milly's disease becomes a refuge from active participation in the world; in effect, Milly takes up her illness as a source of self-definition and security. It is for this reason that she reflects, during her interview with Sir Luke, that her disease "would give her something firm to stand on. . . . It would be strange for the firmness to come, after all, from her learning in these agreeable conditions that she was in some way doomed" (XIX, 236).

Milly's tendency to seek an identity in her fatal illness works both to justify her nonparticipation in life and to provide her with a *modus vivendi*. The passivity she displays from her first appearance in the novel becomes more and more marked after the crucial afternoon at Matcham. Incapable of actively asserting herself in the London world, she views herself as being at the mercy of others and begins almost to invite their victimization of her. For example, at the beginning of the scene in which Kate explicitly warns her to flee from the rapacious crowd of Lancaster Gate (Book V, Chapter 6), Milly reflects that "it pressed upon her then and there that she was still in a current determined, through her indifference, timidity, bravery, generosity—she could scarce say which—by others; that not she but the current acted, and that somebody else always was the keeper of the lock or the dam" (XIX, 274). The sequence of possible explanations for her lack of control—"indifference, timidity, bravery, generosity"—suggests the method by which Milly justifies her passivity; it is, perhaps, "generous" of her that she has made others "the keeper of the lock or the dam." At the same time, however, James seems through this series to emphasize that an equally important motive for Milly's passivity is her less glorious "indifference" to life.

Milly's "timidity," which makes her so vulnerable to the aggressive characters of Lancaster Gate, creates in her—and in the other characters—an oppressive awareness that she is fragile in a world not designed to protect fragility. Thus, just as she welcomes the "firmness" to be found in her fatal illness, so too does she rejoice in the discovery that the world of Lancaster Gate offers the fragile a role to play. When Kate tells her that she is a "dove" (XIX, 283), the image comes to Milly as a key to her nature and as another possible role to adopt: "It was moreover, for the girl, like an inspiration: she found herself accepting as the right one, while she caught her breath with relief, the name so given her. She met it on the instant as she would have met revealed truth; it lighted up the strange dusk in which she had lately walked. *That* was what was the matter with her. She was a dove. Oh *wasn't* she?" (XIX, 283).

The terms with which Milly receives Kate's pronouncement—"*That* was what was the matter with her"—reflects her awareness of a malady of self that corresponds to her malady of body. The beatific qualities associated with the dove are matched by crippling qualities by which the crowd of Lancaster Gate hopes to profit. Milly herself recognizes her dove-like qualities as representative of an affliction and of the reason she does not have access to the ordinary experiences of life—especially the experience of love. It is significant, moreover, that *Kate* is the diagnostician who names for Milly her disease, since it is Kate, with her "talent for life," who so threatens and disturbs Milly. Like the roles offered Milly by other characters in the novel, the role of dove strikes her as both beautiful and useful, and she grasps at it as she has grasped at the roles of princess and American girl because she finds these ready-made identities less painful than living within a complex subjectivity. She learns of the "success she could have as a dove" (XIX, 284), and it soon becomes a part of the repertoire of roles she plays. These roles serve only to alienate Milly ever more greatly from herself and from others.[23]

Increasingly, therefore, Milly turns to her physical illness for the self-definition it might give her. Her belief that she is doomed to die simplifies life enormously for her, as her thoughts during her walk through the London streets, after her visit to Sir Luke, show:

> She had been treated—hadn't she?—as if it were in her power to live; and yet one wasn't treated so—was one?— unless it had come up, quite as much, that one might die. The beauty of the bloom had gone from the small old sense of safety—that was distinct: she had left it behind her there for ever. But the beauty of the idea of a great adventure, a big dim experiment or struggle in which she might more responsibly than ever before take a hand, had been offered her instead. It was as if she had had to pluck off her breast, to throw away, some friendly ornament, a familiar flower, a little old jewel, that was part of her daily dress; and to take up and shoulder as a substitute some queer defensive weapon, a musket, a spear, a battle- axe—conducive possibly in a higher degree to a striking appearance, but demanding all the effort of the military posture. (XIX, 248)

"That one might die" becomes for Milly, as this passage suggests, a possibility that suddenly informs her life with more meaning than it has yet possessed. Further, the threat that life has previously posed to her disappears because the prospect of death renders life only "an experiment" or a "great adventure." Viewed in this way, Milly's life loses consequence; it becomes for Milly a kind of excursion over which she has control, in which she can "more responsibly than ever before take a hand." Participation in life will be analogous to participation in an "experiment"—Milly will become the detached observer of a situation over which she has utter control and which she can always end simply by dying. Milly's health, on which most of life's experiences depend, has been discarded, but the metaphors she uses for it show how inconsequential it has actually been—an "ornament," a "flower," a "little old jewel," a mere "part of her daily dress." Her illness, by contrast, will provide her with a "defensive weapon" which will require of her a "military posture" that will lend her "a striking appearance." The role of a stalwart soldier who encounters pain with a brave resistance becomes Milly's answer to "the practical question of life" (XIX, 250)[24]: "It was perhaps superficially more striking that one could live if one would, but it was more appealing, insinuating, irresistible in short, that one would live if one could" (XIX, 254).

This appeal to Milly of her fatal illness thus explains why Sir Luke's prescription of love cannot be a curative for her. For though he has told her that "to 'live' [is] exactly what I'm trying to persuade you to take the trouble to do" (XIX, 246), Milly ultimately refuses to "take the trouble." She has transformed life, in the sense of direct participation in experience, into an "adventure" and an "experiment" which can have no ultimate or irrevocable consequences. Thus she reflects, when she visits the National Gallery, that she now knows why she had previously shunned museums: "The plea had been explicit—she had done so for life as opposed to learning; the upshot of which had been that life was now beautifully provided for" (XIX, 287). Ironically, however, Milly discovers that she cannot participate even in art; she is attracted not by the masterpieces but by the lady-copyists because "something within her was after all too weak for the Turners and the Titians" (XIX, 288).[25] The lady-copyists also attract Milly because of their third-remove from the vulnerabilities of life,[26] the protective detachment provided them by their imitation of style: "She should have been a lady-copyist—it met so the case. The case was the case of escape, of living under water, of being at once impersonal and firm. There it was before one—one had only to stick and stick" (XIX, 288). This "case of escape" offered by the example of the lady-copyists is one that Milly soon learns to value and adopt, by establishing herself in the museum-like Palazzo Leporelli, that "thorough make-believe of a settlement" (XX, 135).

Sir Luke's insinuation that "love" will save Milly, an insinuation on which, for different reasons, all the other characters base their deceptions of Milly, is an impossible remedy precisely because it involves a vulnerability that Milly is unwilling to risk.[27] Even acknowledging that she "likes" Merton Densher represents to her the one speech "she had ever uttered that cost her most" (XIX, 266). And it is the simple cash basis of her relationship with Eugenio that makes it such a "happy relation" (XX, 133). Eugenio provides services for her, takes care of her problems in return for the money she willingly pays, whereas "Sir Luke had appeared indeed to speak of purchase and payment, but in reference to a different sort of cash. Those were amounts not to be named nor reckoned, and such moreover as she wasn't sure of having at her command. Eugenio—this was the difference—could name, could reckon, and prices of *his* kind were things she had never suffered to scare her" (XX, 142-43). Sir Luke's "prices" do scare Milly because they require a willingness to participate in life, and Milly's fear makes this kind of "cash" unavailable to her. She withdraws into the Palazzo Leporelli, where she eventually becomes so passive that the only "adventure" she wants is "the adventure of not stirring" (XX,148). She provides entertainment for her friends while she herself remains isolated in her palace. She denies genuine intimacy to everyone, though she imitates a kind of intimacy with Kate, for whom she pretends to drop her social facade when they are alone together: "they flourished their masks, the independent pair, as they might have flourished Spanish fans; they smiled and sighed on removing them; but the gesture, the smiles, the sighs, strangely enough, might have been suspected the greatest reality in the business. . . . It was when they called each other's attention to their ceasing to pretend, it was then that what they were keeping back was most in the air" (XX, 138-39).

Though Kate herself has much to conceal from Milly, she is clearly not the only deceptive one of the pair. Kate attributes

Milly's detachment and reserve to her pride that will allow others neither to sympathize with her in her illness nor even openly to acknowledge its existence: "Thus insuperably guarded was the truth about the girl's conception of her validity; thus was a wondering pitying sister condemned wistfully to look at her from the far side of the moat she had dug round her tower" (XX, 139).

Milly's self-chosen and self-established isolation seems to undercut Krook's argument, often endorsed by subsequent critics, that the "inaccessibility of the living to the experience of death and dying is the immediate cause of Milly's tragic deprivation. The living of Lancaster Gate admire and adore Milly Theale; but they withhold from her the one thing that would relieve the terrors of her state—their participation, at once intelligent and generous, in 'the ordeal of consciousness' from hour to hour of a young creature with a great capacity for life condemned to die while hating and fearing death.'"[28] Milly herself to no small extent makes her experience "inaccessible" to the people of Lancaster Gate, despite the evidence that Kate, at least, could and would have participated "intelligently" and "generously" in Milly's "ordeal of consciousness": "It may be declared for Kate, at all events, that her sincerity about her friend, through this time, was deep, her compassionate imagination strong" (XX, 140). With Densher, Milly similarly maintains a detachment by self-consciously acting the role of the American girl. With Susan Stringham, she willingly plays the princess. Thus, as Naomi Lebowitz remarks, Milly does not "strike through her pasteboard mask,"[29] at least not with any of those for whom she cares and to whom she would thereby become vulnerable.

The one person, in fact, with whom she is able to be honest is Lord Mark, and she can allow herself this honesty precisely "because she cared for him so little" (XX, 149). Lord Mark thus becomes in her mind "the one safe sympathiser" (XX, 151), the only character to whom she can utter "her truth" about her fatal illness. To him, also, she tacitly acknowledges that love is not a remedy she is willing to risk:

> "I know what you want."
> Oh, she knew he would know it. But she had brought it

on herself—or almost. Yet she spoke with kindness. "I
think I want not to be too much worried."

"You want to be adored." It came at last straight.
"Nothing would worry you less. . . . It *is* so"—he firmly
kept it up. "You're not loved enough."

"Enough for what, Lord Mark?"

"Why to get the full good of it."

Well, she didn't after all mock at him. "I see what you
mean. That full good of it which consists in finding one's
self forced to love in return." (XX, 156)

Love, Milly recognizes, if it is to be an effective remedy, if one
is "to get the full good of it," requires reciprocity; one cannot
simply *be* loved, one must "love in return." And this "finding
one's self forced to love in return" constitutes such an
enormous threat that Milly can only refuse to see love as a
remedy.

By this point in the novel (the close of Book Seven) Milly
Theale has withdrawn into a psychological state in which she
views both herself and others as objects. Moreover, passivity,
detachment from others, and denial of love as a possible
remedy for her affliction have brought her to an almost total
stasis. This is perhaps the reason for Milly's virtual
disappearance from the last three books of the novel, which are
given over instead to the presentation of her impact on Merton
Densher and of his growing awareness that the immoral
deception he and Kate have practiced on Milly will have
devastating consequences. Clearly, then, though Lord Mark's
revelation to Milly of this deception may constitute the blow
that makes her "turn her face to the wall," it does not
constitute a death blow, for Milly Theale is already dead.

III

An inability or fear seems to prevent James's American girls
from becoming wholly human and from achieving a mature
identity, but Milly Theale represents James's fullest
exploration of the particular features and the possible
consequences of such a fear. Unlike Agatha Grice, whose

inability to establish a self is connected specifically to her brother, Milly Theale is not provided with any direct agent of her affliction. Instead, James seems to seek to establish Milly as a representative American girl who is "the heiress of all the ages." From American men and their singleminded pursuit of wealth she has inherited an unprecedented fortune of "more or less greasy greenbacks," but she has inherited none of the immaterial "cash" she needs to survive. Her inability to achieve a sense of self leads inevitably to her death, and this fact testifies more eloquently even than James's remarks in *The American Scene* to the fact that the American businessman is blighting not simply America, but the American woman as well.

This analysis of Milly Theale does not, of course, represent her character in its entirety, for I have had to ignore the important spiritual dimensions of Milly's character in order to focus on dimensions more pertinent to this study. Though one strand by no means gives an accurate sense of the whole pattern, it can help to illuminate that pattern. My exclusive emphasis here on the psychological can allow us insight into Milly Theale's character that may, perhaps, shed light on the biographical. For what I have suggested is an extreme malady of self in Milly Theale perhaps explains, by analogy, the vehemence of James himself on the subject of the influence of culture on the development of the artist. As we have seen, James felt a close sense of identification with his American girls, whose plight seems to resemble his own as an American artist. And certainly the girl's difficulty in being a subject is analogous to James's own personal situation; for just as her sense of inadequacy is the result of her American background, so, too, James's reasons for his own expatriation lay in the deficiencies, from the artist's point of view, of American culture. It is worth recalling James's response to Howells' criticism of the volume *Hawthorne*.

Howells complained that James had overemphasized the deficiencies of American culture in his biography of Hawthorne, but James protested that these could not be overemphasized because "it is on manners, customs, usages, habits, forms, upon all these things matured and established, that a novelist lives—they are the very stuff his work is made of; and in saying that in the absence of those 'dreary and worn-out paraphernalia' which I enumerate as being wanting in American society, 'we have simply the whole of human life left,' you beg (to my sense) the question. I should say we had just so much less of it as these same 'paraphernalia' represent, and I think they represent an enormous quantity of it."[30] James recognized, then, the consequences for himself as an artist of that "enormous quantity" of life missing in American society; his presentation of Milly Theale points to the analogous consequences of these cultural deficiencies on the development of personality. What is true of Milly Theale is also true, as we have seen, in differing ways and to differing degrees, for James's other American girls: not simply their innocence and goodness but their culturally determined psychology leads to their victimization by the European experience. In his portrayal of Milly Theale, James presents the most extreme form this psychology can take and the most extreme consequences it can have for the American girl. It would be left to Maggie Verver in *The Golden Bowl* to effect an escape from the self-victimization of such a psychology.

6

Transcending Girlhood: Maggie Verver and *The Golden Bowl*

The whole situation works in a kind of inevitable rotary way—in what would be called a vicious circle. The subject is really the pathetic simplicity and good faith of the father and daughter in their abandonment. They feel abandoned, yet they feel consoled, with each other, and they don't see in the business in the least what everyone else sees in it. . . . A necessary basis for all this must have been an intense and exceptional degree of attachment between the father and daughter—he peculiarly paternal, she passionately filial. . . . The other woman and the father and daughter all intensely American.
—*first* Notebook *entry for* The Golden Bowl

I

James's final treatment of the American girl departs
dramatically from the earlier examples, just as *The Golden
Bowl* itself differs dramatically from his earlier fiction, or, for
that matter, from the first two novels of the late phase, *The
Ambassadors* and *The Wings of the Dove*. By far his most
ambitious endeavor, *The Golden Bowl* struck James himself,
while he was completing it, as "the best book, I seem to
conceive, that I have ever done."[1] Although initial sales of the
novel, spurred perhaps by James's concurrent tour of America,
seemed to confirm his estimation, subsequent evaluations
were—and continue to be—less positive. Much of the
discontent readers have experienced with *The Golden Bowl*
stems, it seems, from the difficulty of defining what the novel
is "about"; as John Bayley has observed, "the *subject* of *The
Golden Bowl* cannot be clearly stated, and the problems which
it raises are of the sort which can be solved after a fashion but
which can never be computed; before they can be classified
they have multiplied and mutated themselves endlessly, like
some elemental form of life."[2] The proliferation of
complexities to which Bayley alludes has received little
clarification from James himself; his remarks about *The
Golden Bowl* in the Preface and elsewhere number far fewer
than those on virtually any other of his novels,[3] while it would
seem that *The Golden Bowl* is the novel requiring the most
elucidation.

The moral lines drawn in this novel are also much less clear
than those in *The Ambassadors* or *The Wings of the Dove*. But
while this may account for some readers' distaste for the novel,
the greatest obstacle to understanding seems to be the
difficulties inherent in James's late style, difficulties which
exist at their most intense here. The exasperation experienced
by many readers with these stylistic difficulties was early and
sharply voiced by William James, who wrote to his brother
that the novel had put him

in a very puzzled state of mind. I don't enjoy the kind of "problem" (*viz.*, the adulterous relations between Charlotte and the Prince), and the method of narration by interminable elaboration of suggestive reference (I don't know what to call it, but you know what I mean) goes agin the grain of all my own impulses in writing; and yet in spite of it all, there is a brilliancy and clearness of effect, and in this book especially a high-toned social atmosphere that are unique and extraordinary. Your methods and my ideals seem the reverse, the one of the other—and yet I have to admit your extreme success in this book. But why won't you, just to please Brother, sit down and write a new book, with no twilight or mustiness in the plot, with great vigor and decisiveness in the action, no fencing in the dialogue, no psychological commentary, and absolute straightness in the style.[4]

William's acuteness as a critic asserts itself here, especially in his description of Henry's "method of narration by interminable elaboration of suggestive reference," though from some readers this method elicits as much praise as it does censure from the practical and direct William. Nevertheless, William's grudging acknowledgement of the novel's success resembles not a little the estimate of some contemporary readers; and too often, perhaps, the contemporary reader, like William, loses sight of the fact that the very presence in the novel of those elements he deplores is precisely what makes for the "extreme success" of *The Golden Bowl*.

If *The Golden Bowl* may legitimately be described as James's richest work, it also remains the most resistant in the canon to satisfactory interpretation. In the most valuable study to date of the late novels, Ruth Bernard Yeazell warns that our interpretations of these novels are foredoomed to reductiveness and incompleteness because of the very nature of the late style:

To allow that style fully to work on us is to find ourselves in a world where the boundaries between unconscious suspicion and certain knowledge, between pretense and reality, are continually shifting—in a world in which the power of language to transform facts and even to create them seems matched only by the stubborn persistence of

facts themselves. Necessary as we find it to determine
what are finally truths here, what mere self-deceptions,
and what lies, we do so only by distancing what actually
happens to us as we read these novels—translating them
in the process into safer and less exciting fictions.[5]

The inherent dangers in interpretation that Yeazell describes
are, of course, inevitably multiplied in a study whose focus is
purposely narrow. To single out for analysis the heroine of
any novel always risks violating the novel itself, but that
danger is particularly acute when we approach the heroine of
a novel like *The Golden Bowl*. Though an analysis of Maggie
Verver may momentarily seem to reduce the novel's richness, it
will ultimately, I think, provide a better appreciation of that
richness while at the same time allowing us to see James's
culminating vision of the American girl. Finally, and perhaps
especially with a novel like *The Golden Bowl*, we must
confront the difficulties of interpretation posed by the novel in
something of the same spirit as its author, bearing in mind the
admonishment that James made to himself in *The American
Scene:* "The last thing decently permitted" the critic, he
reminded himself, "is to recognize incoherence—to recognize
it, that is, as baffling; though of course he may present and
portray it, in all richness, *for* incoherence" *(AS,* p. 273).

II

During his tour of America, James was invited to deliver the
1905 Commencement Address at Bryn Mawr; entitling his talk
"The Question of Our Speech," James begged his audience of
young American women to recognize that "all life . . . comes
back to the question of our speech, the medium through
which we communicate with each other; for all life comes back
to the question of our relations with each other."[6] *The Golden
Bowl* attests to the fervency with which James believed in this
idea of the connections between our language and our
relations with each other; certainly the extreme difficulties
posed by the language of the novel are exacerbated by and
reflective of the crucial importance and the complexity of the

"relations" which the four major characters share "with each other."

What distinguishes this novel's heroine from James's earlier American girls is the number and kind of relations she has with the other characters. Far from being bereft like Milly Theale, Maggie Verver is the only one of James's American girls to possess, at the same time, a parent, a husband, and a child.[7] She is also the only one of these American girls not merely to withstand "the whole assault of life" but to triumph over it. Importantly, what in part makes her triumph possible is her eventual renunciation of one of her most valued relations—that with her father, Adam Verver. That this relationship is in fact central to the action was present in James's imagination from his first conception of the novel; the "inevitable rotary" action which leads to "a vicious circle" sprang, James wrote in his *Notebook*, from the "intense and exceptional degree of attachment between the father and daughter."[8] In light of these facts it is surprising that most critics of the novel have not offered psychological analyses of Maggie Verver's character, but have tended to prefer instead a moral or an allegorical perspective. Bayley alone asserts that we should, on the contrary, approach the novel "from the standpoint of personality," rather than "from the standpoint of 'moral values.'"[9] The psychology underlying Maggie Verver's character and her relations with both her father and her husband seems to me particularly essential to our understanding of how and why she alone of James's American girls manages to triumph over life's assault. For that reason, my analysis of her character will forego for the most part any moral assessment of Maggie Verver in the interest of what constitutes, to this study, the more important issue of her psychology.

The key to that psychology resides, as I have noted, in Maggie's relationship with her father, and in this respect James is returning in *The Golden Bowl* to a motif pursued, as we have seen, in much of his short international fiction. Leon Edel and others have argued, with regard to the "exceptional degree of attachment" between Maggie and Adam Verver, that "the 'incestuous' element of father and daughter did not constitute a difficulty" to James.[10] Clearly, however, the psychological dynamics underlying Maggie's attachment to Adam receive little illumination from our reluctance to see that attachment as suggestive of incest even though it is not explicitly incestuous; certainly their attachment seems almost as destructive to its participants as actual incest might be. But the determination to exonerate James from the slightest suspicion of having violated such a formidable taboo has led, it seems, to a critical reluctance to examine the actual dynamics of this relationship. Matthiessen early established the perspective on the relationship that has dominated subsequent critical thought: "James regards this intimacy between father and daughter as 'perfectly natural,' exceptionally close, to be sure, and naively innocent, but without a trace of the pathological fixation that our novelists would now see in it."[11] In fact, however, although Fanny Assingham may protest to Charlotte Stant that Maggie's attachment to Adam is "perfectly natural" (XXIII, 262), the reader should perhaps be as skeptical of Fanny's judgment here as elsewhere in the novel. Certainly one is inclined at various points to agree with Charlotte that "Maggie thinks more on the whole of fathers than of husbands" (XXIII, 257), and to question whether this sort of preference can be regarded as "perfectly natural."

How and why this apparent preference operates may be understood more clearly if we bring to it a perspective offered by R. D. Laing's clinical research into the nature of the "family" and of the relations between family members. Laing, in *The Politics of the Family*, argues that the patterns of thought and behavior established within family structures, that is, "the family as a system," are very early "internalized" by the child, and that this internalized family "may condition, more or less, a person's relationship to himself."[12] Once the "family" has been internalized, moreover, it must not be violated or changed by any member of the family group; as Laing explains, "if self depends on the integrity of the 'family,' the 'family' being a shared structure, self's integrity is then dependent upon self's sense of this as a structure shared with others. One feels secure if one imagines the integrity of the 'family' structure 'in' others."[13]

So crucial to the individual is the continuance of this internalized "family" by each family member that "a crisis will occur if any member of the family wishes to leave by getting the 'family' out of his system, or dissolving the 'family' in himself."[14] Established modes of interaction must thus be maintained because "the 'family' comes to serve as a defence or bulwark against total collapse, disintegration, emptiness, despair, guilt, and other terrors."[15] Even though the individual may wish, for his or her own growth and health, to break away from the "family," to do so proves problematic. On the one hand, "if I do not destroy the 'family,' the 'family' will destroy me"; on the other hand, "I cannot destroy the 'family' in myself without destroying 'it' in them. Feeling themselves endangered, will they destroy me?"[16] Maintaining the "family" thus may frequently seem the only recourse, for as Laing concludes, "the preservation of the 'family' is equated with the preservation of self and world and the dissolution of the 'family' inside *another* is equated with death of self and world-collapse."[17]

Laing's theory of the "politics" that govern family interactions and provide the individual an identity and security seems particularly useful to an analysis of the relationship between Maggie and Adam Verver. That Maggie Verver, in the course of the novel, grows up and learns to prefer her husband to her father may certainly be indisputable; but analysis cannot stop here, as it has so frequently done. For *The Golden Bowl* depicts not simply the birth of the self and its assertion of an autonomous identity, but also the pain, anguish, and difficulty accompanying such a birth—especially for an American girl. And, with acute psychological perceptiveness, the novel dramatizes the deception to which the individual must sometimes resort in order to accomplish that break with the "family."

The "family" shared by Adam and Maggie Verver may be most simply described as their agreement to define themselves almost exclusively in terms of each other. This simple agreement, however, is shown in the novel to have complex and far-reaching effects. For in sharing an identity, instead of having independent identities, they must operate on the assumption that each is responsible for the condition of the other. Maggie assumes responsibility for Adam's happiness and Adam likewise assumes responsibility for Maggie's happiness. One by-product of this sort of engulfment, which leads to the "vicious circle" of their interactions, is, of course, guilt. But more devastating in the novel is the fact that such a mode of relating dooms from the outset Maggie's marriage to Amerigo.

The roots of this "exceptional degree of attachment" between Maggie and Adam would seem to lie in the fact that Maggie's mother, the first Mrs. Verver, died while Maggie was still young. Immediately following Mrs. Verver's death, Adam experiences the epiphany of reaching his "peak in Darien," that is, of discovering that "he had in him the spirit of the connoisseur" and that "a world was left him to conquer and that he might conquer it if he tried" (XXIII, 140-41). This experience occurs "during his first visit to Europe after the death of his wife, when his daughter was ten years old" (XXIII, 142), and from thus early an age Maggie becomes the single and constant companion in his voyage "to rifle the Golden Isles" (XXIII, 141). In this activity Maggie clearly enjoys qualities that, in Adam's mind, his wife lacked;[18] indeed, Adam sees his wife as responsible for his previous lack of "the spirit of the connoisseur": "The futilities, the enormities, the depravities of decoration and ingenuity that before his sense was unsealed she had made him think lovely! . . . he even sometimes wondered what would have become of his intelligence, in the sphere in which it was to learn more and more exclusively to play, if his wife's influence on it hadn't been, in the strange scheme of things, so promptly removed. Would she have led him altogether, attached as he was to her, into the wilderness of mere mistakes?" (XXIII, 143).

Maggie, by contrast with her mother, proves an acceptable companion in Adam's journeys as a collector of art. Adam is, in fact, "conscious of but a single near tie, one affection, one duty deepest-rooted in his life"—his attachment to his daughter (XXIII, 126). This attachment remains unchanged by Maggie's marriage, a marriage to which "he had consented" (XXIII, 147) only because he is able to regard Maggie's husband-to-be as another piece in his collection: "the instinct, the particularly sharpened appetite of the collector, had fairly served as a basis for his acceptance of the Prince's suit" (XXIII, 140). Maggie herself initially shares this attitude toward her husband; moreover, and not surprisingly in view of her attachment to her father, she seems almost to have married the Prince in order to enhance Adam's collection: "'you're at any rate a part of his collection,' she had explained—'one of the things that can only be got over here [in Europe]. You're a rarity, an object of beauty, an object of price'" (XXIII, 12).

Initially, then, Maggie's marriage to Amerigo does little to change her relationship with Adam, in large part because of Amerigo's accommodating "roundness" by which the Prince has "for his father-in-law, while remaining solidly a feature, ceased to be at all ominously a block" (XXIII, 136-37). Maggie and Adam both, clearly, intend that her marriage to Amerigo will make no difference in their own attachment; they have even perversely, "with every ingenuity, converted" Maggie's son "into a link between a mamma and a grandpapa" (XXIII, 156). Despite their absorption of Maggie's marriage into their life together, however, Maggie and Adam are unable wholly to prevent her marriage from effecting a change in Adam's situation: he has now become open to the snares set by fortune-hunting women. Father and daughter's ways of perceiving this change and of dealing with it represent, in fact, the first access James gives us to the psychology underlying their relationship.

Our first direct glimpse of Adam Verver in the novel shows him in retreat from the comically threatening, husband-hunting Mrs. Rance, who seems to Adam "a symbol of the supreme effort that he should have sooner or later, as he felt, to make. This effort would be to say No" (XXIII, 133). Moreover, as he recognizes, "it was Maggie's marriage and Maggie's finer happiness—happy as he had supposed her before—that had made the difference; he hadn't in the other time, it now seemed to him, had to think of such things" because Maggie "had only been his child—which she was indeed as much as ever; but there were sides on which she had protected him as if she were more than a daughter" (XXIII, 134). The repressed anger that so often seems to show itself in this novel here surfaces in the fact that Adam sees his situation made different not simply by Maggie's marriage, but, more interestingly, by her "finer happiness." In regard to the particular issue of Adam's worsened situation, all of the characters—and most importantly Adam and Maggie—proceed on the assumption that Maggie's marriage has, in fact, changed Adam's situation for the worse. But if it is "Maggie's finer happiness" that has created the change, then clearly the important change is not in Adam's situation itself as much as it is in his attitude toward himself and toward Maggie. And his anger towards Maggie would seem to be the catalyst of his new anxiety about the Mrs. Rances of the world; or to put it another way, his anger has been transformed into that anxiety. The actual vulnerability of a man as powerful as Adam Verver to the designs of a Mrs. Rance is surely not in question, nor, surely, does Mrs. Rance motivate Maggie's subsequent behavior. What seems clear from Adam's thoughts here is that he resents the "finer happiness" Maggie has gained from her marriage, in part because "he had supposed her" to be quite happy enough before her marriage—that is, when he and she were completely alone.

But resentment and anger are not feelings permissible in the "family" shared by Adam and Maggie, and thus Adam's new vulnerability to husband-hunting women will be accepted as the reality they have before them. Since this change has been brought about by Maggie, however, both Maggie and Adam think it reasonable that she should somehow deal with that change; as Adam reflects, "if she did at present more [for him] than ever, through having what she called the change in his life to make up to him for, his situation still, all the same, kept pace with her activity—his situation being simply that there was more than ever to be done" (XXIII, 134).

The subsequent anxiety that Maggie feels about Adam—an

anxiety that he himself seems to believe is appropriate—
becomes at one and the same time a sign to both of them that
their relationship has changed and an indication that Maggie
must compensate for that change: "Here of a sudden was a
question that concerned him alone, and the soundless
explosion of it somehow marked a date. He was on her mind,
he was even in a manner on her hands—as a distinct thing,
that is, from being, where he had always been, merely deep in
her heart and in her life; too deep down, as it were, to be
disengaged, contrasted or opposed, in short objectively
presented. But time finally had done it; their relation was
altered" (XXIII, 154). From the moment that both Maggie and
Adam feel that he is "in a manner on her hands," because he
has somehow become "disengaged," the driving force
motivating Maggie is the responsibility she feels to deal with
him, to make up to him for having, through her marriage and
her "finer happiness," changed his situation. Adam's
participation in this is revealed by his persistence in letting her
know how acutely he feels the change, and by his insistence
that he is "on her hands," that he himself lacks the power to
deal with his new situation. Prompted by her guilt and
convinced of her responsibility, Maggie attempts to correct the
situation by promoting his marriage to Charlotte Stant. Much
later in the novel, Maggie reflects to herself that their problems
have all come "from her not having been able not to mind—
not to mind what became of him; not having been able,
without anxiety, to let him go his way and take his risk and
lead his life" (XXIV, 81). Her insight here represents only half
the truth, however, for the early parts of the novel which we
have been examining show that Maggie's anxiety has been
created in part by Adam's own conviction that she is
responsible for him and by his refusal to "take his risk"
himself.

Maggie's attempt to correct the situation created by her own
marriage and "finer happiness" proves, of course, the fatal
error in the novel. She wants Adam to marry because somehow
her own marriage to Amerigo has meant the dissolution of her
"marriage" to Adam: "It was as if you couldn't be in the
market when you were married to *me*," Maggie says to her

father. "Or rather, as if I kept people off, innocently, by being married to you. Now that I'm married to some one else you're, as in consequence, married to nobody" (XXIII, 172). If he should decide to marry, Maggie goes on to say, she wants him to be assured of her "feeling how I've brought you to it. You'll always know that I know it's my fault" (XXIII, 173).

Maggie's desire for her father's marriage seems to originate in her own guilt for having changed his situation, and may represent an effort to assuage that guilt. But the fact that Adam himself does not want to marry,[19] and yet does so to make Maggie feel better, eventually leads to Maggie's feeling that he is, more than ever, "on her hands." One might also argue that Maggie's effort to make Adam marry springs from a small, as yet unconscious desire to have an independent life for herself (and here, as elsewhere in the novel, are distinct echoes of Agatha Grice's situation in "The Modern Warning"); for when, at the beginning of their initial conversation in the garden at Fawns, Adam indicates that Maggie will "see" him "through" the ordeal of saying "no" to fortune-seeking women, Maggie abruptly demands, "why *should* you hold out for ever?" (XXIII, 169). Yet Adam's marriage, because it is designed to make Maggie "positively happy" about Adam (XXIII, 223), and because Maggie knows this from Charlotte Stant herself, results not in greater independence for Maggie but in an exacerbated guilt that forces her to accept whatever "arrangement" of the two couples satisfies Adam.

This oppressive burden of guilt, which Adam helps create, later in the novel contributes to Maggie's fear of telling her father her suspicions about Charlotte and the Prince; she cannot, she reflects, "break the charm" governing their lives because this "charm" keeps Adam "so constantly engaged, so perpetually seated and so contentedly occupied" (XXIV, 34). The psychology underlying Maggie's relationship with her father thus operates to prevent Maggie herself, like so many of James's earlier American girls, from having any kind of independent identity. The mainspring of this psychology is guilt, a guilt which in turn results from the complete responsibility she feels for Adam. And Adam's participation in this "rotary" dynamic, his own desire to maintain the "family" long established with Maggie, helps insure its continued existence. In Laing's terms, both Adam's and Maggie's own "integrity" and "security" of self depend on this "family" they share. Thus, when Maggie's suspicions about Charlotte and the Prince begin to awaken, and she begins, in Fanny Assingham's words, "to doubt, for the first time . . . of her wonderful little judgement of her wonderful little world" (XXIII, 380), the solution will have to be, as Maggie occasionally and fleetingly acknowledges to herself, the destruction of the "family" she shares with Adam.

Its destruction, however, which occupies much of the novel's second volume, cannot be forthrightly named or acknowledged; Maggie must conceal, even to herself, that she is bringing about this destruction. But Maggie's decision "to live" (XXIII, 383) clearly requires her to destroy the kind of bond she shares with her father, though the bond itself requires that she not acknowledge this. Again in Laing's terms, Maggie recognizes that if she does "not destroy the 'family,' the 'family' will destroy" her, inasmuch as she does desire a self connected to her husband and not to her father; at the same time, however, she sees that she "cannot destroy the 'family' in [herself] without destroying 'it' in" Adam. If Adam feels himself "endangered," will he "destroy" her? The only recourse open to Maggie, then, is to behave in such a way that Adam does not suspect that she is destroying the "family" and therefore does not feel himself "endangered." Thus, the adulterous relationship between Charlotte and the Prince is not itself what necessitates the eventual geographic separation of the two couples. Rather, Maggie's destruction of the stultifying bond she shares with Adam can be accomplished only by their geographic separation, for only in that way can the bond be destroyed without any need to acknowledge her own desire for its destruction. This deliberate deception should not blind us, however, to the fact that the process within Maggie which the novel records is in actuality the process of her individuation from Adam, her creation and assertion of a self independent of him.

What provides Maggie with the means of accomplishing selfhood is, of course, her knowledge—her knowledge, that is, of the "real" relations existing between Charlotte and the Prince. This knowledge, because it is "disagreeable," is what, in Fanny Assingham's judgment, causes Maggie's birth as a separate self and makes her "decide to live" (XXIII, 385). Colonel Assingham, through his obtuse conclusion that Maggie will "decide to live—ah yes!—for her child" (XXIII, 386), provokes his wife to explain herself more clearly:

> "Oh bother her child!"—and he had never felt so snubbed, for an exemplary view, as when Fanny now stopped short. "To live, you poor dear, for her father— which is another pair of sleeves!" And Mrs. Assingham's whole ample ornamented person irradiated, with this, the truth that had begun, under so much handling, to glow. "Any idiot can do things for her child. She'll have a motive more original, and we shall see how it will work for her. She'll have to save *him*."
> "To 'save' him—?"
> "To keep her father from her own knowledge. *That*" —and she seemed to see it, before her, in her husband's very eyes—"will be work cut out!" (XXIII, 386)

The suggestions contained in Fanny Assingham's pronouncements are here, as elsewhere in the novel, maddeningly ambiguous.[20] It would seem most immediately clear, for example, that Maggie's decision "to live . . . for her father" hardly represents a new course of action, since her living has always seemed to be "for" him. But the idea of "living for her father" begins at this point in the novel to acquire new meaning. Fanny herself provides two glosses on the notion: Maggie will "have to save" Adam, and this in turn means that she will have "to keep her father from her own knowledge." When we reflect that in the course of the novel Maggie "saves" her father by sending him back to America, "living for her father" assumes a radical redefinition. For what Maggie does is to banish her father under the guise of "saving" him, and she does so in order to destroy the bond between them, thereby making possible a life for her individual self. By telling herself—and others as well—that her behavior is necessary for her father's protection she can finally achieve an independent self.

The Assinghams' conversation makes clear that Maggie's decision "to live" must have a motive outside her own self; Fanny Assingham's words in fact suggest that what we might call the "sacrificial-victim" psychology which has governed Maggie's personality would prevent her from acknowledging a desire "to live" for herself. At the same time, however, living for herself is the actual goal to be achieved, though the means to that goal will be "a motive more original" than "living for her child" would be. And Fanny feels that this means will indeed "work for her": it will felicitously allow Maggie to reach the goal of a life for herself. Thus, "to keep her father from her own knowledge" in order to protect and "save" him will become Maggie's *modus operandi,* just as the very knowledge she will "keep her father from" will function in a practical, daily way to individuate her from him. Keeping "her father from her own knowledge" becomes in the novel Maggie's tool for disentangling her own self from his.[21]

If, however, her knowledge is a "fascination," it is also a "fear" (XXIV, 140), and fear figures prominently among the feelings Maggie experiences about the breaking of the bond with her father. This fear explains in part why she not only blinds herself to the fact that the bond is being broken but also manipulates Adam into being himself the ostensible agent of the break. She cannot herself initiate that action—or, at any rate, she cannot appear, even to herself, to initiate it. She reflects, for example, on the impossibility of communicating to Adam her growing suspicions about Charlotte and the Prince; she cannot communicate that they will

> "do everything in the world that suits us, save only one thing—prescribe a line for us that will make them separate." How could she so much as imagine herself even faintly murmuring that without putting into his [Adam's] mouth the very words that would have made her quail? "Separate, my dear? Do you want them to separate? Then you want *us* to—you and me? For how can the one separation take place without the other?" That was the question that in spirit she heard him ask— with its dread train moreover of involved and connected enquiries. Their own separation, his and hers, was of

course perfectly thinkable, but only on the basis of the sharpest of reasons. Well, the sharpest, the very sharpest, would be that they could no longer afford, as it were, he to let his wife, she to let her husband, "run" them in such compact formation. And say they accepted this account of their situation as a practical finality, acting upon it and proceeding to a division, would no sombre ghosts of the smothered past on either side show across the widening strait pale unappeased faces, or raise in the very passage deprecating denouncing hands? (XXIV, 74)

Almost nightmarish in its final images, this fantasy expresses some of Maggie's deepest fears about her separation from Adam, which she clearly experiences as a threat to her own self. Adam's question about Maggie's desire for their separation rings in her ears as a kind of accusation—perhaps because she does in fact, though unconsciously, desire it. And although she tries to assure herself, in her fantasy, that their separation "was of course perfectly thinkable," the final frightening vision of the fantasy betrays her actual trepidation. Visualizing the life she has shared with Adam as "the smothered past," Maggie acknowledges her own willful participation in its destruction. Thus, she fears that the "sombre ghosts" of both herself and Adam would, from "either side" of the divisive "widening strait," arise and mutually denounce each other. Maggie's deepest fear, then, would seem to be that even the truth about Charlotte and the Prince could not prevent her filial separation from resulting in a haunted and guilt-ridden future. Again, the possible sources of her own guilt are many: guilt for having married; guilt for having persuaded Adam to marry; and, perhaps most terrifying of all, guilt for desiring a life apart from Adam. Although Maggie and Adam do, in fact, engineer their separation without ever acknowledging even the "very sharpest" of reasons, the truth about Charlotte and the Prince, we must wonder to what extent Maggie frees herself from the fears and guilt expressed in this fantasy.

Maggie's relationship with her father, and her struggle to free herself from it, thus almost paradigmatically conforms to the "politics of the family" described by Laing. The situation encountered by Maggie in *The Golden Bowl* and her attempt to deal with it constitute, in Laing's terms, the "crisis" which occurs when "any member of the family wishes to leave by getting the 'family' out of his system, or dissolving the 'family' in himself." Because Maggie can assert "no small self at all" (XXIV, 101), she must resort to a variety of deceptions in her handling of the "crisis" which arises in her life. These deceptions include, for example, persuading Adam to be the agent of their separation: "she tried to focus the possibility of some understanding between them in consequence of which *he should cut loose*" (XXIV, 82; emphasis mine). She must also convince herself that Charlotte and Amerigo are responsible for the necessity of the separation, which, ironically, they in one sense are. She becomes a self-conscious scapegoat to blind herself to the fact that her own desired goal is gradually being realized. And she attempts to conceal "the validity that, like a microscopic insect pushing a grain of sand, she was taking on even for herself" (XXIV, 142)—she attempts to conceal, that is, the autonomous self that she is slowly becoming.

The kinds of deception Maggie employs to dissolve the "family" in herself arise not only from the sorts of fears I have described but also from the ambivalence she feels toward such a dissolution. For destroying the special bond between Adam and herself will not simply give her an independent existence: it will give an independent existence to Adam as well. The fact that she will no longer figure as the most important element in Adam Verver's life seems to create a good deal of the pain Maggie experiences in the last parts of the novel, especially because Charlotte Stant will become her replacement. Her ambivalence also perhaps stems from her fear that she will not be strong enough to live without Adam. These facts help account for certain odd moments in the novel, as, for example, Maggie's response to Fanny Assingham in the following conversation:

> "Is what it comes to that you're jealous of Charlotte?"
> "Do you mean whether I hate her?"—and Maggie thought. "No; not on account of father."

"Ah," Mrs. Assingham returned, "that isn't what one
would suppose. What I ask is if you're jealous on account
of your husband." (XXIV, 110)

A similar indication of Maggie's reluctance to give up her
father arises during her walk with Charlotte during the
famous bridge scene at Fawns; as she and Charlotte look
through the window at Adam, Maggie reflects: "His wife and
his daughter were both closely watching him, and to which of
them, could he have been notified of this, would his raised eyes
first, all impulsively, have responded? in which of them would
he have felt it most important to destroy—for *his* clutch at the
equilibrium—any germ of uneasiness? Not yet since his
marriage had Maggie so sharply and so formidably known her
old possession of him as a thing divided and contested"
(XXIV, 244).

The ultimate expression in the novel of Maggie's
ambivalence about rejecting her special attachment to Adam
occurs, however, in their last conversation together in the
garden at Fawns, when both of them, in fact, work to make
"the present sweet evening" resemble "that other sweet
evening" at Fawns when Maggie first introduced the idea of
bringing Charlotte Stant into their midst:

> It was positively as if in short the inward felicity of their
> being once more, perhaps only for half an hour, simply
> daughter and father had glimmered out for them and
> they had picked up the pretext that would make it easiest.
> They were husband and wife—oh so immensely!—as
> regards other persons; but after they had dropped again
> on their old bench, conscious that the party on the
> terrace, augmented as in the past by neighbors, would do
> beautifully without them, it was wonderfully like their
> having got together into some boat and paddled off from
> the shore where husbands and wives, luxuriant
> complications, made the air too tropical. (XXIV, 255)

If, however, Charlotte and the Prince can seem at this moment
like "luxuriant complications" who make "the air too
tropical," Maggie's nostalgia for the past life she has shared
with Adam does not persist through the end of the novel. In
fact, what gives us our sense of the enormous power Maggie's

relation with Adam has exerted on her life, and what also perhaps works to diminish Maggie's pain in losing him, is the new image in which Adam begins to figure in Maggie's mind. For it is after this evening with Adam in the garden at Fawns, when they have reached the understanding that Adam and Charlotte will move to American City, that Maggie begins to perceive Charlotte's marriage to Adam in this way: "the likeness of their connexion wouldn't have been wrongly figured if he had been thought of as holding in one of his pocketed hands the end of a long silken halter looped round her beautiful neck" (XXIV, 287). This image, troubling readers of *The Golden Bowl* more than any other, has been interpreted as providing various indications of the novel's moral vision.[22] But from the psychological perspective which I have been developing, the image should perhaps be seen as providing us with an understanding of Adam Verver's power over his daughter. Certainly it does not seem farfetched, in light of the engulfing relationship we have seen Maggie trying to free herself from, to argue that the silken noose which now encircles Charlotte Stant's neck once encircled Maggie's. Though Maggie has never recognized the existence of such a noose, the extent to which she can and does sympathize with Charlotte as the prisoner of Adam Verver seems to attest to it. And it is also, perhaps, because Charlotte's neck, not Maggie's, is now in a noose controlled by Adam Verver that Maggie feels at the end of the novel that Charlotte is "dying. Not really, not physically. . . . But dying for us—for you [Amerigo] and me" (XXIV, 346). Whether Maggie is entirely conscious of the price Charlotte Stant pays for her stepdaughter's independence, the novel insists that such is the case. And thus Maggie speaks more truth than she is perhaps aware when she says to the Prince, in the novel's closing chapters, that "it's as if her [Charlotte's] unhappiness had been necessary to us—as if we had needed her, at her own cost, to build us up and start us" (XXIV, 346).

III

Fanny Assingham believes, as I have noted earlier, that Maggie's discovery of the adulterous relationship between Charlotte and Amerigo is the impetus behind her decision "to live," and this belief is often shared by readers of the novel.[23] Charlotte and Amerigo, according to Fanny, will "have *had* to be disagreeable—to show her [Maggie] a little where she is. They'll have had to be disagreeable to make her decide to live" (XXIII, 385). This assessment of what precipitates Maggie's decision "to live" is not, however, altogether accurate. Fanny Assingham herself comes closer to the truth when she observes, earlier in this conversation with her husband, that Maggie has awakened to "the truth that all the while she really *hasn't* had" Amerigo (XXIII, 384). For in fact, a close reading of the opening chapters of the second volume of *The Golden Bowl* reveals that the real impetus which propels Maggie into life, and which also continues to constitute her primary feeling for her husband, is her awakening sexual passion for him. Her decision to act on this passion puts her, in its turn, in a position to discover that something is awry in the relation between Charlotte and the Prince. The action Maggie takes in order to communicate to Amerigo that she has "been so wanting him alone" because the "cup" of her "need" for him has begun "to flow over," has become "too full to carry" (XXIV, 18) is a simple action: she decides to await his return from Matcham (where, ironically, he and Charlotte have consummated *their* passion) in their own home, rather than in Adam's home, where the Prince would, because of the "arrangement" of their lives, naturally expect to find her. This simple action results, however, in her discovery that she is not "playing with blunt and idle tools, with weapons that didn't cut" (XXIV, 9), because the Prince, in his guilt, betrays an "uncertainty" about this break with their normal "arrangement," an uncertainty which initiates Maggie's process of discovery about the adulterous pair. But Maggie's awakened passion for the Prince is the ultimate cause of this discovery process, for her need for him is what prompts her initial disarrangement of the pattern of their lives.

Thus, Maggie's individuation from her father seems to originate in the birth of her sexuality—and James's accuracy here in perceiving the stages of maturation should be noted. Maggie's entry into adulthood springs from the same ground of sexuality which helps prompt this passage in everyone, though her entry is admittedly a delayed one.[24] Although some readers of *The Golden Bowl* have noted Maggie's sexual passion, this passion has not been accorded the significance that its pervasiveness in the novel would seem to demand.[25] Maggie's sexual feelings, and her responses to them, sharply differentiate her from James's earlier American girls.

Becoming aware that her passion for Amerigo "had begun to vibrate with a violence" (XXIV, 7), Maggie reflects that she is merely "like thousands of women, every day, acting up to the full privilege of passion" (XXIV, 8). The problem, however, is that "it had come to the Princess, obscurely at first, but little by little more conceivably, that her faculties hadn't for a good while been concomitantly used" (XXIV, 8). From the reader's standpoint, Maggie's passionate "faculties" have not yet been "used" at all, and the fact that James clearly ties Maggie's birth as an individual self to her awakened passion for the Prince offers perhaps an important gloss on the fear of sexuality and the refusal to live which we saw in Milly Theale. Unlike Milly Theale, Maggie Verver accepts and responds to her passionate "faculties."

Although Maggie responds to her sexual feelings differently than Milly Theale (and, in fact, differently than most of the earlier American girls), what seems to awaken her passion for the Prince is strikingly similar to what awakens Milly Theale. In *The Wings of the Dove*, as we have seen, the sexual presence of "the handsome girl," Kate Croy, creates in Milly Theale a sense of deficiency at the same time that it awakens her to her passionate feelings for Merton Densher, though, as we also saw, she will not acknowledge the nature or even the existence of those feelings. In *The Golden Bowl*, Charlotte Stant exerts an influence on Maggie Verver which is similar to the influence exerted by Kate Croy on Milly Theale. It seems arguable, in fact, that Charlotte Stant not only assumes the silken noose once encircling Maggie's neck, but also impels Maggie into life itself.

Three years older than Maggie Verver, Charlotte Stant initially befriended the young Maggie when they were together in school, and Maggie later considers Charlotte as a potential wife for Adam because she believes that Charlotte is "great in nature, in character, in spirit. Great in life" (XXIII, 180). Even after her own marriage, Maggie recognizes that Charlotte lives in a land of experience which Maggie herself has not glimpsed—and does not want to glimpse.[26] Telling her father, during that important first conversation in the garden at Fawns, that Charlotte "has suffered" because "she has loved—and she has lost" (XXIII, 185), Maggie goes on to acknowledge that she herself has "never had the least blow" (XXIII, 186). She does not know any actual details of Charlotte's suffering, and moreover, "'I wouldn't in any case have let her tell me what would have been dreadful to me. For such wounds and shames *are* dreadful: at least,' she added, catching herself up, 'I suppose they are; for what, as I say, do I know of them? I don't *want* to know!' she spoke quite with vehemence" (XXIII, 187).

One of the superbly ironic movements of *The Golden Bowl* is, of course, Maggie Verver's painful, yet saving, awakening to the knowledge embodied in and acted upon by Charlotte Stant. And that awakening to knowledge begins with Maggie's awakening to her womanhood, which Charlotte also unwittingly, and fatally for herself, assists. For example, Maggie, adorned in her "newest frock," which is "perhaps a little too stiff," anxiously awaits Amerigo's return from Matcham; though she has thus attempted to make herself resplendent for Amerigo, she wonders whether her dress "would at last really satisfy Charlotte" (XXIV, 12-13). The path her mind takes here, in these moments of her excited attendance on Amerigo's return, reveals that Charlotte has somehow awakened Maggie's sense of her femininity:

> She had ever been, in respect to her clothes, rather timorous and uncertain; for the last year above all she had lived in the light of Charlotte's possible and rather inscrutable judgement of them. Charlotte's own were simply the most charming and interesting any woman had ever put on; there was a kind of poetic justice in her being at last able in this particular, thanks to means, thanks quite to omnipotence, freely to exercise her

genius. But Maggie would have described herself as, in these connexions, constantly and intimately "torn"; conscious on one side of the impossibility of copying her companion and conscious on the other of the impossibility of sounding her, independently, to the bottom. Yes, it was one of the things she should go down to her grave without having known—how Charlotte, after all had been said, *really* thought her stepdaughter looked under any supposedly ingenious personal experiment. She had always been lovely about the stepdaughter's material braveries—had done for her the very best with them; but there had ever fitfully danced at the back of Maggie's head the suspicion that these expressions were mercies, not judgements, embodying no absolute but only a relative frankness. Hadn't Charlotte, with so perfect a critical vision, if the truth were known, given her up as hopeless—hopeless by a serious standard, and thereby invented for her a different and inferior one, in which, as the only thing to be done, she patiently and soothingly abetted her? (XXIV, 13-14)

The terms in which Maggie thinks in this passage strongly suggest that not simply her clothes themselves are at stake but her manner of wearing them—and ultimately, her image as a woman. Charlotte is the embodiment and the arbiter of femininity, and Maggie fears that she herself fails to meet Charlotte's standards. And she is in fact correct, since prior to this awakening of her own sexuality she has behaved like a child, not like a woman, with her husband. In much the same way that Milly Theale responds to Kate Croy, Maggie here sharply senses her own inadequacies because of the contrast she feels with Charlotte. The feminine essence which Maggie sees Charlotte as embodying is also, importantly, connected with knowledge: Maggie feels she will "go down to her grave without having known" what Charlotte's judgment of her is. Just as Milly recognized how different she was from Kate, "the handsome girl," so Maggie recognizes her difference from Charlotte. She takes note, on all occasions, of Charlotte's physical presence; for example, when she and Adam return from the Park to Portland Place and she spies Charlotte and Amerigo on the balcony, she notices that Charlotte is "crowned with a brilliant brave hat, responsive to the balmy day, which Maggie immediately 'spotted' as new, as insuperably original, as worn, in characteristic generous harmony, for the first time" (XXIV, 99). Maggie's attention to Charlotte Stant's physical presence, and her tendency to compare herself unfavorably with Charlotte, suggest a kind of jealousy similar to that we saw at work in Milly Theale.

These stirrings of jealousy generated in Maggie by Charlotte Stant's physical attractiveness do not, however, lead Maggie to withdraw from the arena.[27] Maggie's response, unlike Milly Theale's, is to awaken to her own physical self and her sexual passions. She determines, moreover, that she will not allow Charlotte to continue to regard her as existing in "a different and inferior" category, just as she determines that she will no longer be kept in a "bath of benevolence" because "baths of benevolence" are appropriate only for "a patient of some sort, a nervous eccentric or a lost child" (XXIV, 44). Maggie determines, that is, to count, to be recognized by others as an adult woman, and this determination makes her the only one of James's American girls really to transcend the title of "girl." Maggie becomes angry, in fact, about her previous dependent, infant-like status and decides to take action to change it. For example, when she imagines Lady Castledean's perception of her as a strange sort of woman to be the wife of Amerigo, we can detect behind her language an anger that will eventually lead her to change the "arrangement" of her life:

> There was something in Amerigo to be explained, and she was passed about, all tenderly and expertly, like a dressed doll held, in the right manner, by its firmly stuffed middle, for the account she could give. She might have been made to give it by pressure of her stomach; she might have been expected to articulate with a rare imitation of nature, "Oh yes, I'm *here* all the while; I'm also in my way a solid little fact and I cost originally a great deal of money." (XXIV, 51)

The very fact that Maggie has become interested in and sensitive to the perceptions which others have of her indicates that something within her has begun to live—and, as my discussion has suggested, that "something" includes a new awareness of her sexuality, an awareness which seems in large part to have been created by Charlotte Stant's presence.

This new awareness in Maggie makes possible that individuation of herself from Adam which I discussed earlier. The "family" she has shared with Adam has resulted, as we have seen, in the engulfment of her self in his. But if Adam is for Maggie a figure whose power over her, through the special "family" they have shared, prevents her from having an independent self, her husband is a figure differently but equally powerful. Maggie's awakened passion for the Prince constitutes the primary, if not almost the only, way in which she experiences him. In virtually every instance in the novel's second volume her thoughts of or encounters with Amerigo contain some reference to the sexual desire she feels for him. Yet, as several critics of the novel have noted,[28] Maggie's very passion for the Prince provides him with enormous power over her, especially when he attempts to respond to her passion with his own. His passion puts her "in his power" (XXIV, 28); it produces in her "a sort of terror of . . . weakness" (XXIV, 29); resisting it requires "an effort that horribly hurt her" (XXIV, 57) because she knows she possesses (like Isabel Archer) an "endless power of surrender" (XXIV, 352). Thus, though Maggie acknowledges and accepts her own sexual feelings, in ways that serve to distinguish her from James's earlier American girls, she is nevertheless fearful of yielding to them.

Yeazell argues that this fear originates in the perception that "sexual surrender . . . [is] identical with the loss of all conscious control."[29] Thus, she continues, in *The Golden Bowl* "sexual passion becomes the central mystery, the hidden knowledge which the Jamesian innocent must at last confront."[30] Within the context of my discussion, however, Maggie's fear of yielding to her sexual passion would seem to be explicable in somewhat different terms. In fact, Maggie's fear perhaps indicates that she already intuits "the hidden knowledge" contained in sexual passion. As we have seen, the principal psychological drama of *The Golden Bowl*, from the point of view of its heroine, involves Maggie's individuation from her father, her birth as an independent and autonomous self. The power exerted by that attachment to Adam makes her birth as a self enormously difficult, frightening, and painful. If what makes her separation from Adam at all possible is the equally powerful force of her sexual passion for her husband, that passion itself has been made possible, as we have seen, by her awakening to her own womanhood, which is an integral aspect of the identity of her newly born self. To yield to her passion for the Prince would, however, threaten Maggie's struggle for an autonomous self, which I would argue is an indication that she correctly intuits the symbolic meaning embodied in such a yielding. Maggie rightly recognizes—and, of course, James her creator rightly recognizes—that she must establish a strong and secure sense of self before her yielding to her passion for Amerigo can cease to threaten her. For just as Maggie feels that she has "no small self at all" with her father, she also feels that she has "no small self at all" with her husband (XXIV, 101). What she must do, then, is somehow free herself from her engulfing relationship with Adam without simply shifting to a different but equally engulfing relationship with Amerigo.

That this interpretation corresponds to Maggie's own understanding of the change occurring in her life is amply supported by the novel. For example, very early in Maggie's journey to selfhood, Amerigo attempts to woo her away from the glimmerings of new knowledge which he suspects he spies in her; his method of wooing her is, of course, through his "unfailing magic," that act which Maggie feels always "operated with him *instead* of the words he hadn't uttered— operated in his view as probably better than any words, as always better in fact at any time than anything" (XXIV, 29). When he resorts to his "unfailing magic" this time, however, Maggie recognizes that "whatever he might do she musn't be irresponsible. Yes, she was in his exerted grasp, and she knew what that was; but she was at the same time in the grasp of her conceived responsibility, and the extraordinary thing was that of the two intensities the second was presently to become the sharper" (XXIV, 56). As their ride home together continues, Maggie becomes aware that to give up "her conceived responsibility," that is, to abandon her journey to knowledge (which is also her journey to selfhood), by simply surrendering to the Prince's—and her own—passion, would be to "give up everything for ever" (XXIV, 56). If Maggie is finally to reach knowledge and to achieve a sense of herself as a separate being, she must postpone her surrender to passion. Only after she has achieved a strong and secure sense of self can she enter a full relationship with another and not lose herself.

For many readers, the most compelling aspect of the novel's second volume is, in fact, Maggie's assertion of a self, her making of herself a personage with whom the other characters must "reckon." The manipulations and deceptions which she practices on the others have, however, been so fully documented and explored by critics of the novel that little is to be gained by reviewing them once more.[31] But from the psychological perspective of our discussion, Maggie's transformation from the victim into a kind of victimizer would seem to be necessitated by two important forces. The first, which I have discussed at some length, is her need to conceal from her father that the "family" they share must, for her own birth as a self, be destroyed. The second force involves the nature of the world Maggie inhabits. Though readers of the novel have noticed that Maggie essentially beats the other characters at their own game, and proves, in fact, a superior player, they have not often recognized that for Maggie to achieve the status of a subject in the world to which she awakens she *must* learn to play the game of that world. Thus, if she learns to manipulate appearances instead of naively continuing to believe in their reality,[32] she does so because those are the terms of the world she confronts.

The pain which Maggie's successful assertion of herself creates for the others, and in particular for Charlotte, is thus in some senses unavoidable. More important, however, though Maggie recognizes and even sympathizes with that pain, she does not allow it to block her own behavior. As Yeazell points out, "the direct link between imaginative sympathy and self-sacrifice . . . is in *The Golden Bowl* strangely broken," a fact which accounts, Yeazell says, for "much of the moral disquiet which this novel arouses in us."[33] The truth which James

seems to be asserting in *The Golden Bowl* is that the claims of
the self, especially when the very survival of the self is at stake,
must ultimately take precedence over the claims of the other.
That James should articulate such a truth through the figure
of his last American girl has important implications for the
present study, as we will see; but our uneasy suspicion that this
truth does underlie much of the novel's action also perhaps
explains why readers have tended to admire the self-sacrificing
Milly Theale much more than the self-asserting Maggie
Verver—some psychological necessities are, in fact, morally
disturbing.

If James does insist on the claims of the self, however, his
understanding of the difficulties and the pain encountered
when the self chooses life is nowhere more acute than in *The
Golden Bowl*. To the very end of the novel, he does not flinch
from showing the price the self must pay for its own existence.
That price and Maggie Verver's awareness of it are, in fact,
what make the novel's ending tragic. Maggie's assertion of
herself throughout the second half of the novel has had as its
ultimate goal a life with Amerigo that is independent of and
separate from Adam and Charlotte; more than this, Maggie
has also worked, though not entirely consciously, to insure
that her life with Amerigo will be a life of two individual
selves, not a life in which she loses herself, through her
passion for him, to Amerigo. When on the closing pages of the
novel Adam and Charlotte have taken their final leave of
Maggie and Amerigo, Maggie reflects that

> everything now, as she vaguely moved about, struck her
> as meaning so much that the unheard chorus swelled. Yet
> *this* above all—her just being there as she was and
> waiting for him [Amerigo] to come in, their freedom to
> be together always—was the meaning most disengaged:
> she stood in the cool twilight and took in all about her
> where it lurked her reason for what she had done. She
> knew at last really why—and how she had been inspired
> and guided, how she had been persistently able, how to
> her soul all the while it had been for the sake of this end.
> Here it was, then, the moment, the golden fruit that had
> shown from afar; only what *were* these things in the fact,

for the hands and for the lips, when tested, when tasted—
what were they as a reward? Closer than she had ever been
to the measure of her course and the full face of her act,
she had an instant of the terror that, when there has been
suspense, always precedes, on the part of the creature to
be paid, the certification of the amount. Amerigo knew it,
the amount; he still held it, and the delay in his return,
making her heart beat too fast to go on, was like a sudden
blinding light on a wild speculation. (XXIV, 367)

When Amerigo does return, Maggie's "terror" at first
disappears, because "his presence alone, as he paused to look
at her, somehow made it the highest, and even before he had
spoken she had begun to be paid in full" (XXIV, 368). But in
the next moment Maggie becomes aware that the "meaning"
of her act may be different to Amerigo than it is to her; she
suddenly senses that Amerigo thinks she is "waiting for a
confession. This in turn charged her with a new horror: if *that*
was her proper payment she would go without money"
(XXIV, 368).

The "horror" of a confession from Amerigo would seem to
arise from the fact that such a confession would remind them
both that their new life together has been "at the expense of
Charlotte" (XXIV, 368). Attempting to dispel this realization
of the price Charlotte has had to pay, Maggie reminds the
Prince of Charlotte's ability to rise to the demands and
possibilities of her new life in America by asking him, "Isn't
she too splendid?" (XXIV, 368). The fact that Charlotte is so
"splendid" is crucial, as Maggie tries to explain:

> "That's our help, you see," she added—to point further
> her moral.
> It kept him before her therefore, taking in—or trying
> to—what she so wonderfully gave. He tried, too clearly,
> to please her—to meet her in her own way; but with the
> result only that, close to her, her face kept before him, his
> hands holding her shoulders, his whole act enclosing her,
> he presently echoed: "'See'? I see nothing but *you*." And
> the truth of it had with this force after a moment so
> strangely lighted his eyes that as for pity and dread of
> them she buried her own in his breast. (XXIV, 368-69)

What Maggie comes to realize in this closing passage of the novel would seem to be the cost of her assertion of self. For though Charlotte is "splendid," though she will make a life for herself in America, she also will live with Adam Verver's silken noose around her neck, enduring, too, all the while, the pain of losing the man she has so passionately loved. She pays, in a sense, part of the price of Maggie's new selfhood. And Amerigo here, though indifferent to Charlotte's pain, seems charged with his recognition of Maggie as the agent of that pain. Maggie, in turn, realizes that Amerigo's recognition of her power is really a recognition of her complicity—not just in rearranging the lives of all of them but in evil itself. From having "no small self at all" with the Prince, Maggie has moved to having a very large and powerful—and also tainted—self with him. Her achievement of selfhood has brought with it, inevitably James seems to insist, her complicity in an ever-recurring Fall. Something like a recognition of this truth is thus perhaps what "lights" the Prince's eyes, making Maggie bury "her own in his breast."

IV

My analysis of Maggie Verver's drama in *The Golden Bowl*, though it has of necessity ignored other important aspects of this wonderfully rich novel, does provide an avenue for a fuller understanding of two important elements in James's conception of the American girl: his sense of the connections between the American male, whose values shaped American culture, and the plight of the American girl; and his perception of why the American girl has thus functioned as the mere "embroidery" on the "canvas" of the American male. Through Maggie Verver's attachment to Adam, James makes clear that if his earlier American girls were unable to take "the whole assault of life" it is because they possessed no real self with which to encounter it. Furthermore, through Maggie and Adam, James demonstrates more completely than he had done before that this lack of a self results from the total dominance of the American male and his values. Only by disentangling

herself from the "family" she shares with Adam can Maggie
Verver achieve selfhood—thereby becoming the only one of
James's American girls to transcend the decorative status of
"embroidery" on another's "canvas."

To transcend that status Maggie must destroy the "family"
she shares with Adam, and, as we have seen, expel Adam from
her world.[34] It is crucial that we understand Adam Verver and
his values in order to understand what James felt had to be
banished for the American girl to flourish.[35] Though, as we
have seen, James had depicted and deplored in his earlier
fiction and nonfiction the materialistic values which he saw as
endemic to America, in Adam Verver—the wealthiest
American of them all—he suggests the most insidious effects
which these values can have on those whose lives are touched
by them. Adam Verver's acquisitiveness, which is perhaps his
most distinctive quality, drives him to acquire not only a
fortune and then the art masterpieces of the world, but his
daughter's very soul. Though most readers have recognized
Adam Verver's habit of viewing the Prince and Charlotte as
objects to be bought and then exhibited, no reader to my
knowledge has seen that a similar attitude informs his
relationship with his daughter. There seems simply to be no
room in Adam's world for a subjective self other than his own;
he is an "I" living, as he thinks, in a world populated entirely
by "its." And this absolute egoism seems, from James's
characterization of Adam, to result from his wholly
materialistic values. Adam's talent for success in the only
arena America finds worthwhile, the marketplace, leads him
to believe that the acquisition of money empowers him to
acquire anything, including wives and sons-in-law. But, of
course, such a habit of viewing the world essentially
dehumanizes every person—including his daughter—in that
world.[36] We must not, therefore, underestimate the importance
of Maggie's expulsion of Adam from her life.[37]

Adam Verver's treatment of Charlotte and the Prince as
objects leads in the novel to their similar treatment of Maggie
and Adam; all four become "pieces" to be "arranged" in ways
agreeable to them all. Maggie's struggle for selfhood may be
seen as a struggle to transform herself from an object into a

subject. Adam, the ultimate arranger of her world, must thus be made "to cut loose" so that she can in fact function as a subject. Yet the sort of ruthlessness required to effect such a transformation is understandably something that many readers have found morally disturbing. As we noted earlier, however, psychological and moral imperatives often conflict, and nowhere more profoundly perhaps than in this novel. From a strictly psychological perspective it is clear that Maggie's decision "to live," to become an independent self, quite simply necessitates a violence toward and at times a violation of others; her decision in itself is, in fact, a violation against the world she inhabits, for that world—consisting of Charlotte, Amerigo, and Adam, each with different motives—prefers that she not live at all, that she remain a manipulable or decorative object.

This subject-object antithesis is given emphasis in the novel through the developing opposition of connoisseur and artist. The connoisseurship which dominates Adam Verver's life and speech is particularly significant when it is considered alongside the metaphors of artistry consistently used in the novel's second volume to characterize Maggie's achievement of selfhood. Though both sets of metaphors have been noticed by students of the novel,[38] no one has considered them in conjunction with each other. The danger inherent in being a connoisseur was for James, according to Viola Hopkins Winner, that it could become "a sign of a wrong, an arbitrary relationship to the past if the collector or connoisseur views art purely aesthetically and acquisitively, not as the expression of human life."[39] Maggie Verver in the first volume of the novel seems to share with Adam this sort of attitude toward art, an attitude which extends to people. It is thus surely significant that James describes Maggie's emerging selfhood as her transformation into an artist, a creator. She moves from being at once an object and a collector of objects to becoming a subject and a creator. And to thrive as a creator, an artist, she must reject Adam, the ultimate connoisseur.

James's presentation of Maggie as an artist who must struggle free from her stultifying relationship with Adam of course suggests a strong autobiographical element at work in

The Golden Bowl. One feels that James's own necessity to break with America and its values in order to become the artist he wished to be underlies much of the drama of this novel and much of the identification he seems to have felt with his American girls. Yet it is also this element that accounts for part of the unrest readers experience with Maggie Verver. For Maggie is not in any ordinary sense an artist; the materials for her art are human lives, not language or paint or marble. And here we feel that James once again confronts the problem we saw at work in *The Portrait of a Lady.* There he endowed his heroine with the responsive imagination which he associated with both the artist and the feminine personality; here, he goes further and characterizes his heroine explicitly as an artist. But in neither case is his heroine actually an artist, and therein lies the problem. For though James seems in *The Golden Bowl* to be trying to make an important distinction between Adam the connoisseur and Maggie the artist, that distinction fails to work in a wholly positive way because the reader cannot uncritically accept the medium of Maggie's "art" as a morally legitimate one.

Ultimately, however, James's failure to make Maggie an unquestionably attractive heroine would seem to stem from his perception that a fully triumphant American girl must inevitably surrender her innocence and goodness, and thereby an essential part of her attractiveness. As we have seen, Isabel Archer determines to live with evil but she does not thereby forfeit her own essential goodness. Maggie Verver's experience is of a very different sort. For Maggie Verver finally opens her eyes to knowledge and accepts the suffering accompanying it, but then goes one step further: she determines that her own self and her own desires must, if they are to be realized, take precedence over the selves and desires of others, and, in acting on that determination, she acknowledges her willingness to enter a fallen world and share its taint. As the Prince tells her, "everything's terrible, cara—in the heart of man" (XXIV, 349), and Maggie, at the end of the novel, recognizes and accepts her own complicity in evil.

By doing so, she becomes, ironically perhaps, James's greatest tribute to the American girl, for by doing so she alone of his American girls escapes the culturally created psychology that has crippled the others. Stephen Spender long ago pointed out that "in James's other books he has convinced us that a part of life, of the *real* life of a human being as apart from the performance of an automaton, is the power to choose to die. The question James has not yet answered is whether it is possible in the modern world to choose to live: and Maggie triumphantly answers it for him."[40] Maggie's decision to live entails a counterattack on "the whole assault of life" which, while it taints her, also attests to James's belief that this is the only way one can become fully human.

If readers have tended to prefer James's earlier American girls to Maggie Verver, that is perhaps because these earlier American girls, though they are psychologically crippled, retain an essential innocence and goodness that are absent from the fallen world most of us inhabit. Because she realizes that to live she must enter that fallen world, Maggie Verver perhaps seems too little like a heroine of fiction, too much like ourselves. For Maggie is no longer the beautiful and graceful "embroidery" on another's "canvas," but has herself become an embroiderer.

Notes
Bibliography
Index

Notes

Chapter 1

1　*The Notebooks of Henry James,* ed. F. O. Matthiessen and Kenneth B. Murdock (New York: Oxford University Press, 1947), p. 47.
2　Patricia Stubbs, *Women and Fiction: Feminism and the Novel, 1880-1920* (London: Methuen, 1979), pp. 5, 9.
3　Julia Kristeva has remarked that not only the novel but "writer and literature in general are considered feminine" in Western culture. See "Oscillation Between Power and Denial," trans. Marilyn A. August, in *New French Feminisms,* ed. Elaine Marks and Isabelle De Courtivron (Amherst: The University of Massachusetts Press, 1980), p. 166.
4　See Mary Doyle Springer, *A Rhetoric of Literary Character: Some Women of Henry James* (Chicago: The University of Chicago Press, 1978) and Edward Wagenknecht, *Eve and Henry James: Portraits of Women and Girls in His Fiction* (Norman: University of Oklahoma Press, 1978).
5　William Dean Howells, "Mr. Henry James's Later Work," in *The Question of Henry James: A Collection of Critical Essays,* ed. F. W. Dupee (London: Wingate, 1947), p. 27.
6　J. P. Mowbray, "The Apotheosis of Henry James," in *Henry James: The Critical Heritage,* ed. Roger Gard (New York: Barnes & Noble, 1968), p. 331.
7　F. W. Dupee, *Henry James* (1951; rpt. New York: William Morrow, 1974), p. 97.
8　Dupee, *Henry James,* p. 97. An acquaintance of James, Ehrman Syme Nadal, who was the Second Secretary of the American Legation in London for a brief period of time, also noted James's

identification with women during his early years in London: "He seemed to look at women rather as women looked at them. Women look at women as persons; men look at them as women. The quality of sex in women, which is their first and chief attraction to most men, was not their chief attraction to James." See Leon Edel, *Henry James; The Conquest of London, 1870-1881* (Philadelphia: Lippincott, 1962), p. 359. Later in James's life, this quality continued to impress, as is attested by Desmond McCarthy: "I remember being struck . . . by how much woman there seemed to be in him. . . . It struck me that women ran on in talk with him with a more unguarded volubility than they do with most men, as though they were sure of his complete understanding." See Simon Nowell-Smith, *The Legend of the Master* (London: Constable, 1947), p. 86.

9 Philip Rahv, "The Heiress of All the Ages," in *Image and Idea: Twenty Essays on Literary Themes*, rev. ed. (Norfolk, Conn.: New Directions, 1957), p. 57.

10 Theodore Roszak, "The Hard and the Soft: The Force of Feminism in Modern Times," in *Masculine/Feminine: Readings in Sexual Mythology and the Liberation of Women*, ed. Betty Roszak and Theodore Roszak (New York: Harper & Row, 1969), p. 92. Roszak suggests that this "compulsive masculinity" was actually a response to "the quickening tempo of the women's rights movement as it comes down from the 1830's and 1840's" (p. 93).

11 Lisa Appignanesi, *Femininity and the Creative Imagination: A Study of Henry James, Robert Musil, and Marcel Proust* (London: Vision Press, 1973), p. 14. Appignanesi defines the "feminine imagination" as one that creates "an art of which the two distinguishing features are interiorization and the conscious creation of mystery either around or within the work of art. The long historical insistence on the otherness of woman, her core of feminine mystery, makes her the natural focus for an art which finds no fruitful material in what it considers the prose of ordinary life and which seeks to transcend the configurations of a known reality" (p. 15).

12 Henry James, *The American Scene*, ed. Leon Edel (Bloomington: Indiana University Press, 1968), pp. 455, 164; hereafter referred to as *AS*.

13 Henry James, *The Art of the Novel*, ed. R. P. Blackmur (New York: Scribners, 1962), p. 5; all citations to the Prefaces to the New York Edition are to this collection, hereafter referred to as

AN. Another interesting example of James's use of the metaphor to describe his art occurs in *Notes of a Son and Brother*, where he says that the reader "will accuse me of treating an inch of canvas to an acre of embroidery. Let the poor canvas figure time and the embroidery figure consciousness—the proportion will perhaps then not strike us as so wrong." See *Henry James: Autobiography*, ed. Frederick W. Dupee (London: W. H. Allen, 1956), p. 521.

14 William Dean Howells, *Heroines of Fiction* (New York: Harper, 1901), II, 165-66.

15 Rahv, "Heiress of All the Ages," p. 51.

16 William Wasserstrom, *Heiress of All the Ages: Sex and Sentiment in the Genteel Tradition* (Minneapolis: University of Minnesota Press, 1959), p. 52.

17 Paul John Eakin, *The New England Girl: Cultural Ideals in Hawthorne, Stowe, Howells, and James* (Athens, Ga.: University of Georgia Press, 1976), p. 5.

18 Nina Auerbach, *Communities of Women: An Idea in Fiction* (Cambridge, Mass.: Harvard University Press, 1978), pp. 122-23.

19 *Autobiography*, p. 268. Donald L. Mull offers an analysis of the biographical origins of James's attitude toward money and the businessman in *Henry James's "Sublime Economy": Money As Symbolic Center in the Fiction* (Middletown, Conn.: Wesleyan University Press, 1973), pp. 3-13.

20 *Henry James: Letters, 1843-1875*, ed. Leon Edel (Cambridge, Mass.: Belknap-Harvard University Press, 1974), I, 228.

21 *Autobiography*, p. 283.

22 *Letters*, I, 219.

23 *Letters*, I, 231.

24 *Autobiography*, p. 283.

25 *Letters*, I, 226.

26 See Paul Bourget's description of "Les Femmes et Les Jeunes Filles" in America in his work *Outre-Mer* (Paris: Alphonse Lemerre, 1895), I, 99-150.

27 Martha Banta, in her analysis of *The American Scene*, argues that in fact the "American male has wed his business," and that his legal wife is in reality only "his mistress." See "They Shall Have Faces, Minds, and (One Day) Flesh: Women in Late Nineteenth-Century and Early Twentieth-Century American Literature," in *What Manner of Woman: Essays on English and American Life and Letters*, ed. Marlene Springer (New York: New York University Press, 1977), pp. 235-70.

28 Banta, "They Shall Have Faces," p. 238.
29 For an account of James's itinerary, see Leon Edel's Introduction and Notes to his edition of *The American Scene.*
30 James's description conforms closely to Freud's description of the brothel's symbolic representation in dreams. See *The Interpretation of Dreams* in *The Standard Edition of the Complete Psychological Works of Sigmund Freud,* trans. James Strachey (London: Hogarth and the Institute of Psycho-Analysis, 1953), V, 354.
31 Henry James, *French Poets and Novelists,* introd. Leon Edel (New York: Grosset & Dunlap, 1964), p. 320.

Chapter 2

1 Ferner Nuhn, *The Wind Blew from the East* (New York: Harper Bros., 1940), p. 104.
2 My discussion of Lacan's ideas is based upon *Ecrits: A Selection,* trans. Alan Sheridan (London: Tavistock, 1977) and *The Four Fundamental Concepts of Psycho-Analysis,* trans. Alan Sheridan, ed. Jacques-Alain Miller (London: The Hogarth Press & The Institute of Psycho-Analysis, 1977).

Lacan's opaque style makes short, direct quotation from his work difficult. For this reason I have drawn extensively from the best commentary in English on Lacan's ideas: Anthony Wilden, "Lacan and the Discourse of the Other," in *The Language of the Self: The Function of Language in Psychoanalysis* by Jacques Lacan, trans. Anthony Wilden (New York: Dell, 1968), pp. 159-311. I am indebted to Wilden's commentary for the considerable light it sheds on Lacan's texts.

For a more general introduction to and discussion of Lacan's ideas, the reader is referred to Malcom Bowie's essay, "Jacques Lacan," in *Structuralism and Since: From Lévi-Strauss to Derrida,* ed. John Sturrock (New York: Oxford University Press, 1979), pp. 117-40.
3 Lacan's conception of the child's discovery of the Other is derived from Freud's discussion of the infant's game of disappearance and return in *Beyond the Pleasure Principle.* See *Standard Edition,* XVIII, 15-20.
4 Wilden, "Lacan and the Discourse of the Other," p. 191.
5 Shoshana Felman, "Turning the Screw of Interpretation," *Yale French Studies,* 55/56 (1977), 112.

6   Wilden, "Lacan and the Discourse of the Other," p. 190.

7   Ibid., p. 290.

8   For a discussion of Euphemia de Mauves as a forerunner of the later Isabel Archer see Rebecca Patterson, "Two Portraits of a Lady," *Midwest Quarterly*, 1 (1960), 343-61.

9   Except where otherwise noted, all references throughout this book to the fiction of Henry James are to *The Novels and Tales of Henry James*, New York Edition, 24 vols. (New York: Scribners, 1908-9). Parenthetical page references in the text, preceded by a Roman numeral volume number, will be to this edition.

10 J. A. Ward offers a fine and detailed discussion of Madame de Mauves' fear of pain, and also indicates this as a motivation of her behavior: "It is not a question of scruples withholding her from adultery, but of fears withholding her from the experience of pain." See *The Search for Form: Studies in the Structure of James's Fiction* (Chapel Hill: University of North Carolina Press, 1967), p. 189.

11 *Henry James: Letters, 1875-1883*, ed. Leon Edel (Cambridge, Mass.: Belknap-Harvard University Press, 1975), II, 303.

12 Christof Wegelin divides James's American girls into two types. The first type struggles with "limitations on her freedom imposed from without," the second with "the growth of her awareness." Although Wegelin's classification has a certain descriptive use, indicating the structure of the fiction in which the American girl appears, it does not provide much clarity with regard to the American girl's psychology. See *The Image of Europe in Henry James* (Dallas: Southern Methodist University Press, 1958), p. 69.

13 Eakin asserts that "for the James heroine it is her imagination that confers upon her a New England identity" (p. 133), and argues that the development of the fully imaginative heroine is tied both to James's shift in focus from the observer of the girl to the girl herself, and to James's recognition of his need for a heroine "with precedents." See pp. 131-67 of *The New England Girl* for a discussion of the intellectual background of this heroine.

14 The exceptions to this are Bessie Alden of "An International Episode" and Agatha Grice of "The Modern Warning," both of whom are pretty and imaginative.

15 It is also interesting to note, however, that a lack of physical beauty awakens in Milly Theale and Maggie Verver a sense of

inner inadequacy, a sense to which Milly responds by dying, and to which Maggie responds by deciding to be born as a self. See Chapters Five and Six for discussions of how this functions for each of them.

16 *Notebooks*, p. 128.
17 Henry James, "The Speech of American Women: Part I," *Harper's Bazar*, November 1906, p. 980.
18 Ibid., p. 980.
19 Ibid., p. 982.
20 Henry James, "The Manners of American Women: Part IV," *Harper's Bazar*, July 1907, p. 648.

Chapter 3

1 See the entry for 23 October 1891 in the *Notebooks*, p. 116.
2 The Freudian revisionist Karen Horney points out that this sort of insatiable desire to acquire material goods stems from the fact that "greedy persons distrust their capacity to create anything of their own, and thus have to rely on the outside world for the fulfillment of their needs; but they believe that no one is willing to grant them anything." This idea has an obvious and important relevance to the American girl's inadequate sense of self, as my discussion will go on to make clear. See *The Neurotic Personality of Our Time* (New York: Norton, 1937), p. 126.
3 For a sociopsychological analysis of these character traits shared by Mr. Dosson and most of James's other American businessmen, see David Riesman, *The Lonely Crowd: A Study of the Changing American Character* (New Haven: Yale University Press, 1950). Riesman discusses extensively the shift from the "inner-directed" man who dominated nineteenth-century American society to the "outer-directed" modern man who has emerged in the twentieth century. Reisman's descriptions of the values and behavior of the "inner-directed" man provide a useful gloss on James's fictionalized American businessmen.
4 This sexlessness is not, of course, peculiar to the American girl in James's fiction, or even to his female characters, though it is more common in his female Americans than in his female Europeans. There are certainly similarly sexless male characters, such as Lambert Strether and John Marcher. But James's use of psychosexual immaturity to figure other sorts of immaturity seems especially pronounced in his various treatments of the American girl.

5 Henry James, *The Europeans: A Sketch* (Boston: Houghton Mifflin, 1878), p. 109. James excluded *The Europeans* from the New York Edition of his work.

6 Henry James, "The Modern Warning," in *The Complete Tales of Henry James,* ed. Leon Edel (Philadelphia: Lippincott, 1963), VII, p. 49. Subsequent references are in the text. James excluded this tale from the New York Edition of his work.

7 A number of details in "The Modern Warning" attest to the strong sense of identification James felt with his American girls. Agatha Grice, like James, is of Irish descent. By his decision that he would have to leave America in order to realize his artistic ambitions, James, like Agatha, incurred the disapproval of many of his countrymen. And though James succeeded in asserting his own identity, while his American girl of this story fails, this success could not have come easily. As Edel has pointed out, William James tended to disparage his brother's decision to be a writer by suggesting "that the pen wasn't a normal instrument for an American." William also, from their childhood on, attempted to imply that Henry was not as "masculine" as his older brother, which Edel argues may not have been "so much a relegation of Henry to a feminine role as to a kind of second-class citizenship." The two were, of course, more or less identical in the nineteenth century. See *Henry James: The Conquest of London,* pp. 156-58, 384-86.

8 Martha Banta, *Failure and Success in America: A Literary Debate* (Princeton: Princeton University Press, 1978), p. 359.

9 A notable exception to this critical tendency is James D. Wilson's "The Gospel According to Christopher Newman," *Studies in American Fiction,* 3 (1975), 83-88.

10 Daniel Schneider, *The Crystal Cage: Adventures of the Imagination in the Fiction of Henry James* (Lawrence, Kansas: The Regents Press of Kansas, 1978), pp. 44-45.

11 *Letters,* II, 105.

12 See the entry for 26 November 1892 in the *Notebooks,* p. 129.

13 Banta also notes that Newman is an "excellent example of the 'masculine' factor" *(Failure and Success,* p. 376). For a discussion of Newman as an archetypal American, see R. W. Butterfield's *"The American,"* in *The Air of Reality: New Essays on Henry James,* ed. John Goode (London: Methuen & Co, 1972), pp. 5-35.

14 Citations in my text from *The American* refer to the Riverside Edition, ed. Matthew J. Bruccoli, with an Introd. by Roy Harvey Pearce (Boston: Houghton Mifflin, 1962). This is a reprint of the 1879 (first authorized English) edition, with twenty-eight

emendations by Bruccoli. The New York Edition of *The American* differs markedly from the first edition, and although a scholarly debate continues over the respective merits of the two editions, I agree with Pearce that the original edition is the better novel because in the New York Edition "Newman is endowed with a kind of sensibility which is simply inappropriate to his conduct and character" (xviii).

15 Richard Poirier, *The Comic Sense of Henry James: A Study of the Early Novels* (New York: Oxford University Press, 1967), p. 64.

16 Edel, *Henry James: The Conquest of London*, pp. 249-50.

17 Susan P. Ward, "Painting and Europe in *The American*," *American Literature*, 46 (1975), 572. Mull also argues that James inherited from his father the idea that if one possesses "the business imagination" then "one's relation to other persons will generally parallel one's relation to things" *(Henry James's "Sublime Economy,"* p. 9). Despite his "conversion" before he came to Europe, Newman seems in the novel quite definitely possessed of such a "business imagination."

18 Karen Horney, "Inhibited Femininity," in *Feminine Psychology* (New York: Norton, 1967), p. 82.

19 *The Diary of Alice James*, ed. Leon Edel (London: Rupert Hart-Davis, 1965), p. 96.

Chapter 4

1 Quoted in Edel, *Henry James: The Conquest of London*, p. 402.

2 Eakin also discusses this shift and offers a fine analysis of the intellectual background of Isabel's character. See *The New England Girl*, pp. 133-94.

3 James discusses in the Preface the fact that the extreme difficulty of this task has led writers like Dickens and Scott simply to avoid it; and even such writers as Shakespeare and George Eliot, who have attempted it, have never allowed their heroines "to be sole ministers" of the "appeal" of their themes. James's own goal in the *Portrait* was to make Isabel Archer such a "sole minister," that is, to center the novel on her. See *The Art of the Novel*, pp. 49-52.

4 Some theoreticians of the novel argue that in order for fiction to become "emphatically psychological" the novelist has to turn away from the methods of realistic fiction. See, for example,

Maurice Z. Schroder, "The Novel As A Genre," in *The Theory of the Novel*, ed. Philip Stevick (New York: The Free Press, 1967), p. 27.

5 T. S. Eliot was the first to observe that James shared with Hawthorne a quest for the "deeper psychology." See his essay, "On Henry James: In Memory," in Dupee, *The Question of Henry James*, p. 130.

6 William Veeder, in *Henry James: The Lessons of the Master* (Chicago: University of Chicago Press, 1975), offers an exhaustive treatment of the ways in which the *Portrait* addresses the condition of women in the 1870s. Elizabeth Sabistan, in a comparative analysis of the provincial heroine in *Emma*, *Madame Bovary*, *Middlemarch*, and *The Portrait of a Lady*, argues that "the final and inescapable prison for all four women is neither the provinces nor marriage nor ignorance, but the prison of womanhood." See "The Prison of Womanhood," *Comparative Literature*, 25 (1973), 336-51.

7 Horace E. Scudder, rev. of *Portrait*, *The Atlantic Monthly*, January 1882, pp. 27-28; rpt. in the Norton Critical Edition of *The Portrait of a Lady*, ed. Robert D. Bamberg (New York: Norton, 1975), p. 652.

8 In her article, "Revision and Thematic Change in *The Portrait of a Lady*," *Modern Fiction Studies*, 22 (1976), 183-200, Nina Baym argues that "to assume that Isabel ought to marry because she is female is to beg one of the major questions raised by her story" (p. 195). Though Baym rightly offers a corrective to those critics who have believed that Isabel should marry, she fails to note that while the novel does not endorse the validity of this assumption, it does realistically place Isabel in a world where such an assumption underlies the structure of society. Judith Fryer, in *The Faces of Eve: Women in the Nineteenth-Century American Novel* (New York: Oxford University Press, 1976), more accurately states that because Isabel "is a woman, her choice is limited, finally, to which of her possible suitors she will marry" (p. 128).

9 F. W. Dupee helped establish some of the bases of my thinking about the novel in his provocative statement that marriage "figures in the *Portrait* not as a specific social institution . . . but as a condition of existence—of Isabel's existence in particular." See his *Henry James*, p. 104.

10 Naomi Lebowitz, in *The Imagination of Loving: Henry James's Legacy to the Novel* (Detroit: Wayne State University Press,

1965), claims that the Jamesian novel can in fact be defined as "the novel of personal relationships" (p. 14).

11 Henry James, *The Question of Our Speech; The Lesson of Balzac: Two Lectures* (Boston: Houghton Mifflin, 1905), p. 10.

12 *Letters*, I, 226. Leon Edel claims that this statement reflects James's personal relief at not having "to marry Minny and risk the awful consequences." See *Henry James: The Untried Years, 1843-1870* (Philadelphia: Lippincott, 1953), p. 331.

13 Oscar Cargill is the only major critic who disputes the relation of Isabel Archer to Minny Temple. His primary reason for doing so is to correct the notion that Isabel is an ideal character, a notion which he believes stems from seeing her in relation to James's cousin. See *The Novels of Henry James* (New York: Macmillan, 1961), pp. 82-83. Since James himself did not see Minny as an ideal figure, however, her fictional sisters, including Isabel Archer, need hardly be ideal either. See my discussion of Minny Temple in Chapters One and Five.

The two most exhaustive studies of the connections between Minny Temple and Isabel Archer are: Ernest Sandeen, *"The Wings of the Dove* and *The Portrait of a Lady:* A Study of Henry James's Later Phase," *PMLA*, 69 (1954), 1060-75; rpt. in *Perspectives on James's The Portrait of a Lady*, ed. William T. Stafford (New York: New York University Press, 1967), pp. 187-205; and Lotus Snow, "The Disconcerting Poetry of Mary Temple: A Comparison of the Imagery of *The Portrait of a Lady* and *The Wings of the Dove*," *New England Quarterly*, 31 (1958), 312-39.

14 *Letters*, II, 174.

15 *Letters*, II, 314.

16 This idea is further supported by the fact that all of the major characters except two—Ralph Touchett and Caspar Goodwood—are, or have been, married. Significantly, Ralph's stated reason for not marrying is his lung disease, which guarantees him but a short tenure in life (III, 259); and Caspar Goodwood's stubborn refusal to consider his life in connection with any woman other than Isabel marks him as a character unwilling or unable to accept or commit himself to the conditions of life.

17 For an excellent analysis of the ways in which the various marriages function in the plot and themes of the novel, see Laurence Bedwell Holland, *The Expense of Vision: Essays on the Craft of Henry James* (Princeton: Princeton University Press, 1964), pp. 3-54.

18   Quentin Anderson, *The American Henry James* (New Brunswick, N.J.: Rutgers University Press, 1957), p. 195.

19   That expert in social realities, Madame Merle, confirms Isabel's judgment in this matter when she warns Isabel that while "it's a very good thing for a girl to have refused a few good offers" of marriage, Isabel should not "keep on refusing," especially since she is "not what is technically called a *parti*" (III, 289-90).

20   Discussions that do take into account the importance of Isabel's attitude toward her fortune are Baym's "Revision and Thematic Change in *The Portrait of a Lady*"; Mull's *Henry James's "Sublime Economy,"* pp. 48-115; and Eugene L. Stelzig's "Henry James and the 'Immensities of Perception': Actors and Victims in *The Portrait of a Lady* and *The Wings of the Dove*," *Southern Humanities Review*, 11 (1977), 253-65.

21   Sandeen suggests that in the *Portrait* "James betrays an idealist's anxiety to justify his heroine's wealth. Isabel must first prove her great qualities and when she has passed the test to the satisfaction of all who observe her . . . she is rewarded as people like her undoubtedly deserve to be but seldom are" (p. 192). Given the changes in her character that her fortune creates, however, I suspect that other artistic motives may be at work.

22   Baym, "Revision and Thematic Change in *Portrait*," 196.

23   It is interesting to note in regard to Isabel's feelings of guilt that in the chapter immediately following Osmond's proposal, Isabel visits, at his request, his daughter Pansy. A dominant motif in Pansy's innocent prattling is her father's poverty, which, Pansy realizes, complicates her own eventual marriage since "it costs so much to marry!" (IV, 28).

24   Mary S. Schriber, in "Isabel Archer and Victorian Manners," *Studies in the Novel*, 8 (1976), 441-57, believes that Isabel consciously "usurps the power of the male" (p. 453). As my discussion indicates, such an assertion must be considered in light of the guilt which this reversal of sexual roles creates in Isabel. Her feelings about the masculine power that her fortune gives her are clearly ambivalent. And, it is hardly the case that "Isabel's marriage to Osmond is a marriage of Titans" (p. 453).

William Bysshe Stein argues that rather than showing a reversal of sexual roles created by Isabel's inheritance, the novel instead depicts Isabel from beginning to end as betraying her essential "womanhood" and as victimized by her "sterile femininity." Stein believes that it is the "world created by male ingenuity" that has corrupted the female and that prevents her from continuing to shape "her life in accordance with the demands of nature." Instead, "her ardors are inflamed by the affectation of thought, not by the fever of blood." See *"The Portrait of a Lady: Vis Inertiae," Western Humanities Review,* 13 (1959), 177-90; rpt. in Stafford, *Perspectives on James's The Portrait of a Lady,* pp. 166-83. My discussion of the novel clearly begins from a different set of assumptions about the nature of sexual roles. For a specific argument against Stein's interpretation of the novel, see Annette Niemtzow, "Marriage and the New Woman in *The Portrait of a Lady," American Literature,* 47 (1975), 377-95.

25   Among the harshest of Isabel's critics on this point are Schriber; Leon Edel, "Introduction" to *The Portrait of a Lady* (Boston: Houghton Mifflin, 1963), pp. xii-xiii; and Marjorie Perloff, "Cinderella Becomes the Wicked Stepmother: *The Portrait of a Lady* as Ironic Fairy Tale," *Nineteenth-Century Fiction,* 23 (1969), 413-33.

26   John Roland Dove offers a sound argument against those interpretations that view Isabel as being afraid of intimate relationships, and claims that, on the contrary, Isabel before her marriage possesses a "belief in the redemptive powers of a personal relationship," and that at the end of the novel she "recognizes the idea of a perfectly reciprocal relationship as a myth." See his "Tragic Consciousness in Isabel Archer," *Studies in American Literature,* Louisiana State University Studies, Humanities Series No. 8, ed. Waldo McNeir and Leo B. Levy (Baton Rouge: Louisiana State University Press, 1960), pp. 78-94.

27   The importance of the process of perception in the *Portrait* is discussed by Dorothy Van Ghent, *The English Novel: Form and Function* (1953; rpt. New York: Harper & Row, 1961), pp. 211-28.

28   Martha Banta, *Henry James and the Occult: The Great Extension* (Bloomington: Indiana University Press, 1972), pp. 171, 170. Banta argues that James, in this aspect of his treatment of Isabel, indicates his general agreement with his father's ideas about knowledge: "According to Henry James, Sr., experience is a prerequisite for gaining knowledge. To possess knowledge means one has learned the difference between good and evil; to learn the difference between good and evil demands that one has suffered the experience of each" (p. 170).

29   For a discussion of Ralph's moral culpability see William H. Gass, "The High Brutality of Good Intentions," *Accent,* 18 (Winter, 1958), 62-71; rpt. in Stafford, *Perspectives on James's The Portrait of a Lady,* pp. 206-16.

30 See Leon Edel, *Henry James: The Middle Years, 1882-1895* (Philadelphia: Lippincott, 1962), p. 305.

31 Fryer finds Isabel to be, in the terms used by James to describe Hawthorne's Zenobia, his "nearest approach to the creation of a *person*" (p. 126).

Chapter 5

1 In a letter written in the Fall of 1902, to be found in F. O. Matthiessen, *The James Family* (New York: Knopf, 1948), p. 338.

2 Dorothea Krook also notes that Milly's disease is both "physical and spiritual," but she concludes that Milly's spiritual malady is the "lonely, loveless condition" which results from her being too pure for this world. See *The Ordeal of Consciousness in Henry James* (Cambridge: Cambridge University Press, 1962), p. 214.

3 See Psalms 55.

4 See, for example, Quentin Anderson, *The American Henry James*, pp. 234-80; Millicent Bell, "The Dream of Being Possessed and Possessing: Henry James's *The Wings of the Dove*," *Massachusetts Review*, 10 (1969), 97-114; R. W. B. Lewis, "The Vision of Grace: James's *The Wings of the Dove*," *Modern Fiction Studies*, 3 (1957), 33-40; and Christof Wegelin, *The Image of Europe in Henry James*, pp. 106-21.

5 *Autobiography*, p. 544.

6 *Letters*, I, 232.

7 *Autobiography*, p. 283.

8 *Autobiography*, p. 283.

9 *Letters*, I, 219.

10 *Letters*, I, 228, 224.

11 *Autobiography*, p. 544.

12 *Letters*, I, 222.

13 *Letters*, I, 223-24.

14 *Autobiography*, p. 509.

15 *Letters*, I, 222.

16 *Letters*, I, 224.

17 This is William Dean Howells' wonderful phrase, to be found in his essay, "Mr. Henry James's Later Work," p. 36.

18 Such an approach has been taken by Robert C. McLean, "'Love by the Doctor's Direction': Disease and Death in *The Wings of the Dove*," *Papers on Language and Literature*, 8, supplement (1972), 128-48. McLean attempts to prove that "a sexually frustrated Milly Theale" (p. 130) commits suicide "most

probably by leaping to her death from the balcony of the Palazzo Leporelli" (p. 128). Such an approach seems to me to be so reductive of the richness of James's portrayal of Milly Theale as to contribute little to our understanding and appreciation of that portrayal.

19 F. O. Matthiessen, *Henry James: The Major Phase* (New York: Oxford University Press, 1944), p. 64.

20 Full discussions of the parallels in the novel between Kate Croy and Milly Theale are offered by Holland, *The Expense of Vision*, pp. 316-27; and Ward, *The Search for Form*, pp. 166-99.

21 Miriam Allott, "Symbol and Image in the Later Work of Henry James," *Essays in Criticism*, 3 (1953), 327.

22 Lacan, following Freud, would point out that the desire for unity and harmony is in fact a desire for death.

23 Holland reaches a different conclusion about Milly's adoption of roles, which he argues reflects her "gain in self-possession" and by which she "begins to mold" the world of Lancaster Gate (p. 298). Similarly, Kenneth Graham believes that "Milly's roles are active and organic" and that they are to be viewed positively; see his discussion in *Henry James: The Drama of Fulfillment* (London: Oxford University Press-Clarendon, 1975), pp. 160-201. As my discussion shows, however, the novel suggests that Milly's roles have negative rather than positive effects on her because the "self-possession" she gains is the self-possession of stasis and death.

24 My reading of Milly's character is supported by the fact that this phrase from the novel clearly echoes James's description of his sister Alice's tragic illness; as I noted earlier, James called his sister's illness "in a manner the only solution for her of the practical problem of life." See Edel, *Henry James: The Middle Years*, p. 305.

25 Another interesting parallel with Alice James surfaces in Milly's being "too weak for the Turners and the Titians," for Alice wrote in her journal (with which, after her death in 1892, James was completely familiar) that "I can't read anything suggestive, or that survives, or links itself to experience, for it sets my silly stomach fluttering, and my flimsy head skipping so that I have to stop." See *The Diary of Alice James*, p. 50.

26 A similar point is made by John Goode, who concludes, however, that "Milly's apotheosis is achieved not by becoming a picture, but by becoming a consummate tourist." See his excellent essay, "The Pervasive Mystery of Style: *The Wings of the Dove*," in *The Air of Reality*, pp. 244-300.

27   James's psychological acumen in proposing love as a cure for Milly's illness has of course been revealed by Freud's work. Freud argues in "On Narcissism" that "in the last resort we must begin to love in order not to fall ill, and we are bound to fall ill if, in consequence of frustration, we are unable to love" *(Standard Edition,* XIV, 85).

28   Krook, *The Ordeal of Consciousness,* p. 213.

29   Lebowitz, *The Imagination of Loving,* p. 76.

30   *Letters,* II, 267.

Chapter 6

1   Henry James to J. B. Pinker, 20 May 1904, in *The Letters of Henry James,* ed. Percy Lubbock (New York: Scribners, 1920), II, 15.

2   John Bayley, *The Characters of Love: A Study in the Literature of Personality* (London: Constable, 1960), p. 210.

3   Leon Edel indicates that perhaps a major reason for the brevity of James's remarks about *The Golden Bowl* in its Preface was his disappointment over initial sales of the New York Edition of his works. Edel quotes Theodora Bosanquet, who noted that James was "depressed" over the sales figures and that he had "nearly finished *Golden Bowl* preface—bored by it—says he's 'lost his spring' for it." See Leon Edel, *Henry James: The Master, 1901-1916* (Philadelphia: Lippincott, 1972), p. 434.

4   This letter may be found in Matthiessen, *The James Family,* p. 339.

5   Ruth Bernard Yeazell, *Language and Knowledge in the Late Novels of Henry James* (Chicago: University of Chicago Press, 1976), p. 3.

6   James, *The Question of Our Speech,* p. 10.

7   Maggie's possession of these three primary relationships has also been noted by Appignanesi, who argues that this fact makes Maggie "the fullest feminine in James's fictional canvas." See *Femininity and the Creative Imagination,* p. 72.

8   See the entry for 28 November 1892 in the *Notebooks,* pp. 130-31.

9   Bayley, *The Characters of Love,* p. 214.

10   Edel, *Henry James: The Master,* p. 210. Edel also draws attention to the probable impact on James of a similar relationship between Francis and Lizzie Boott. After Lizzie Boott's marriage to the artist Frank Duveneck, Lizzie continued the close relationship with her father and "Duveneck had seemed to James very much of a third party" (p. 211).

11 Matthiessen, *The Major Phase*, pp. 92-93.

12 R. D. Laing, *The Politics of the Family and Other Essays* (New York: Vintage-Random House, 1969), pp. 4, 8.

13 Ibid., p. 13.

14 Ibid., p. 14.

15 Ibid., p. 14.

16 Ibid., p. 14.

17 Ibid., p. 14.

18 Wasserstrom places the Maggie-Adam relationship within the context of father-daughter relationships in American literature. He also notes the contribution of Maggie to Adam Verver's conversion, a contribution made possible by her being both "nymph and nun." Wasserstrom, however, gives short shrift to the psychological dynamics of their relationship. See *Heiress of All the Ages*, pp. 84-98.

19 There is ample evidence in *The Golden Bowl* that Adam does not himself desire marriage but marries Charlotte to make Maggie feel better. Adam reflects, for example, when threatened by Mrs. Rance, that he would not like having to say "no" to a husband-hunting woman, but that "he knew himself, however, well enough not to doubt: he knew coldly, quite bleakly, where he would, at the crisis, draw the line" (XXIII, 134). Later, in conversation with Maggie, he speaks as though marriage *"might be an idea"* if it came from her and was something she wanted (XXIII, 171). He also says, in response to Maggie's apparent desire that he marry, "you're . . . not *so* ready, to see me through my resistance [to marriage]?" (XXIII, 174). Later, when he decides to propose to Charlotte, he reflects that to consider marriage "merely for himself would have been, even as he had just lately felt, even doing all justice to that condition—yes, impossible. But there was a grand difference in thinking of it for his child" (XXIII, 208-9). Such an accumulation of evidence in the novel thus invalidates the assumption made by Cargill that Maggie mistakenly believes Adam married for her sake. See *The Novels of Henry James*, pp. 408-9.

20 Yeazell astutely discusses the role of Fanny Assingham in *The Golden Bowl*, and points out that "in Fanny, James mocks the elaborate evasiveness with which his characters so often speak, even while he dramatizes in moving terms the crucial purposes which such language serves. The voice of William James is permitted to intrude into the world of *The Golden Bowl* [through Colonel Assingham] and to invite us to laughter at its

expense; but though we are allowed our measure of mockery, even the jester is finally silenced and converted" *(Language and Knowledge,* p. 97).

21 J. A. Ward also points out that Maggie's knowledge "necessitates" an isolation from her father. See *The Imagination of Disaster* (Lincoln: University of Nebraska Press, 1961), p. 152. Yeazell almost anticipates my argument when she observes that "to confront her father directly is a risk which the Princess cannot bear to take: it is as if she feared that knowing the truth about him might paralyze her entirely" (p. 120).

22 Some typical conclusions about this image include the following: Cargill says the image "is not objective evidence of Adam Verver's cruelty but of Maggie's awakening pity" *(The Novels of Henry James,* p. 405); Matthiessen states that James fails to acknowledge the "cruelty" of the image and that this failure "is nothing short of obscene" *(The Major Phase,* p. 100); Philip M. Weinstein finds appalling Maggie's "failure to reassess her father" after having this vision of him; see *Henry James and the Requirements of the Imagination* (Cambridge, Mass.: Harvard University Press, 1971), p. 177.

23 One critic, in fact, goes so far as to aver that Charlotte and the Prince do not actually commit adultery but simply "conspire together" to force the separation of Maggie and Adam. See John A. Clair, *The Ironic Dimension in the Fiction of Henry James* (Pittsburgh: Duquesne University Press, 1965), pp. 79-102.

24 Yeazell observes that the adults in James's late fiction experience "a crisis remarkably like that of adolescence" and that "in the children of the 1890s James directly anticipates the bewilderment of his twentieth-century adults" (p. 34).

25 Yeazell is an important exception here; though she does not give extensive attention to the role of Maggie's passion in the novel, she shows the importance of such passion in the late fiction in general. She argues, in fact, that "the sexual reticence of his late fiction is in direct proportion to the felt presence of sexuality as a force at the very center of human life" (p. 20).

26 My use of Blakean terms here is deliberate, for it seems that *The Golden Bowl* has further parallels with Blake's *The Book of Thel* than merely in the possible allusion of the novel's title to that poem's motto, a parallel noticed by numerous readers ("Does the eagle know what is in the pit, / Or wilt thou go ask the Mole? / Can Wisdom be put in a silver rod? / Or Love in a golden bowl?"). Blake's Thel, a virgin who is brought out of the

land of innocence into the land of experience, flees "shrieking" after her initial glimpse of the horrors of the land of experience. The initiation she refuses is, of course, in part a sexual one. Maggie Verver seems, in the first half of the novel, analogous to Thel, as do many of James's earlier American girls; unlike Thel, however, Maggie chooses to dwell in the land of experience once her sight has been opened to it.

27   It is also worth noting that James endows Charlotte Stant with greater physical beauty than he provides Maggie Verver. As Fanny Assingham remarks to her husband, Prince Amerigo has had, in Charlotte and Maggie respectively, the "enjoyment" of "one beautiful woman—and one beautiful fortune" (XXIV, 129). For further descriptions of the physical characteristics of Charlotte and Maggie, see: XXIII, 46-47; XXIII, 187-88; XXIII, 245; XXIII, 266-67.

28   See, for example, Weinstein, *The Requirements of the Imagination*, pp. 168-69 and 181-82; and Yeazell, *Language and Knowledge*, pp. 18-22.

29   Yeazell, *Language and Knowledge*, p. 19.

30   Ibid., p. 20. Yeazell contends that this is the case for all of James's novels from *What Maisie Knew* through *The Golden Bowl*.

31   Among the significant analyses of Maggie's manipulations and deceptions, the following provide a balanced overview: Leo Bersani, *A Future for Astyanax: Character and Desire in Literature* (Boston: Little, Brown, 1969), pp. 128-55; David Mogen, "Agonies of Innocence: The Governess and Maggie Verver," *American Literary Realism*, 9 (1976), 231-42; Gabriel Pearson, "The Novel to End All Novels: *The Golden Bowl*," in Goode, ed., *The Air of Reality*, pp. 301-62; Sallie Sears, *The Negative Imagination: Form and Perspective in the Novels of Henry James* (Ithaca, N. Y.: Cornell University Press, 1968), pp. 153-222; and Charles Thomas Samuels, *The Ambiguity of Henry James* (Urbana: University of Illinois Press, 1971), pp. 210-26.

32   Sears also makes note of this change in Maggie's attitude toward appearances *(The Negative Imagination,* p. 213).

33   Yeazell, *Language and Knowledge*, pp. 114, 115.

34   Several critics, including Yeazell, have felt that in the closing chapter of the novel Maggie still shares in Adam Verver's reductive attitude toward Charlotte and the Prince. They have viewed as particularly offensive the exchange between Adam and Maggie as they look at their *sposi* as "human furniture"; in response to Adam's *"Le compte y est. You've got some good*

things," Maggie says, "Ah, don't they look well" (XXIV, 360).

I believe, however, that my discussion requires us to re-evaluate the extent to which this exchange illustrates the idea that Maggie still shares Adam's aesthetic perspective on human beings. As my analysis of Maggie's process of individuation from Adam indicates, Maggie can effect her separation from Adam only by pretending that she does not want to do so and by concealing from him that she is achieving an independent identity of her own. It should also be noted that even in the earlier parts of the novel, Maggie expresses such an attitude only in conversation with or about Adam Verver.

35 For good character analyses of Adam Verver, see Frederick C. Crews, *The Tragedy of Manners: Moral Drama in the Later Novels of Henry James* (New Haven: Yale University Press, 1957; rpt. Hamden, Connecticut: Archon-Shoe String, 1971), pp. 81-114; and Wasserstrom, *Heiress of All the Ages*, pp. 90-96.

36 Mull points out that the person with a "business imagination" is likely in James's fiction to regard people as things: "people will become commercial entities, objects possessed by one's self, and, as possessions, the concrete definitions of the self. The business imagination is thus an attitude toward all aspects of life, an attitude which determines the self's loss in its appurtenances and relations." Mull goes on to argue, however, that Adam Verver, like Christopher Newman, has been "converted" from the "business imagination" (*Henry James's "Sublime Economy,"* pp. 9, 136). The seriousness and permanence of this conversion are, of course, hotly disputed by readers of the novel, which suggests a deliberate ambiguity on James's part. As my discussion indicates, I am among those who remain unconvinced of Adam's conversion.

37 Christof Wegelin does recognize the necessity of Adam's expulsion; he sees Adam as representative of "a stage in the American relation to Europe which must be purged." See *The Image of Europe in Henry James*, p. 126.

38 See, for example, Mark L. Krupnick, "*The Golden Bowl:* Henry James's Novel About Nothing," *English Studies*, 57 (1976), 533-40; and Elsa Nettels, "The Scapegoats and Martyrs of Henry James," *Colby Library Quarterly*, 10 (1974), 413-27.

39 Viola Hopkins Winner, *Henry James and the Visual Arts* (Charlottesville: The University Press of Virginia, 1970), p. 166.

40 Stephen Spender, *The Destructive Element* (London: Jonathan Cape, 1935), p. 89.

Bibliography

Allott, Miriam. "Symbol and Image in the Later Work of Henry James." *Essays in Criticism*, 3 (1953), 321-36.

Anderson, Quentin. *The American Henry James.* New Brunswick, N. J.: Rutgers University Press, 1957.

Appignanesi, Lisa. *Femininity and the Creative Imagination: A Study of Henry James, Robert Musil, and Marcel Proust.* London: Vision Press, 1973.

Auerbach, Nina. *Communities of Women: An Idea in Fiction.* Cambridge, Mass.: Harvard University Press, 1978.

Banta, Martha. *Failure and Success in America: A Literary Debate.* Princeton: Princeton University Press, 1978.

Banta, Martha. *Henry James and the Occult: The Great Extension.* Bloomington: Indiana University Press, 1972.

Banta, Martha. "They Shall Have Faces, Minds, and (One Day) Flesh: Women in Late Nineteenth-Century and Early Twentieth-Century American Literature." In *What Manner of Woman: Essays on English and American Life and Literature.* Ed. Marlene Springer. New York: New York University Press, 1977, pp. 235-70.

Bayley, John. *The Characters of Love: A Study in the Literature of Personality.* London: Constable, 1960, pp. 205-62.

Baym, Nina. "Revision and Thematic Change in *The Portrait of a Lady.*" *Modern Fiction Studies*, 22 (1976), 183-200.

Bell, Millicent. "The Dream of Being Possessed and Possessing: Henry James's *The Wings of the Dove.*" *Massachusetts Review*, 10 (1969), 97-114.

Bersani, Leo. *A Future for Astyanax: Character and Desire in Literature.* Boston: Little, Brown, 1969.

Bourget, Paul. *Outre-Mer.* 2 vols. Paris: Alphonse Lemerre, 1895.

Bowie, Malcom. "Jacques Lacan." In *Structuralism and Since:*

From Lévi-Strauss to Derrida. Ed. John Sturrock. New York: Oxford University Press, 1979, pp. 117-40.

Butterfield, R. W. "The American." In *The Air of Reality: New Essays on Henry James.* Ed. John Goode. London: Methuen, 1972, pp. 5-35.

Cargill, Oscar. *The Novels of Henry James.* New York: Macmillan, 1961.

Clair, John A. *The Ironic Dimension in the Fiction of Henry James.* Pittsburgh: Duquesne University Press, 1965.

Crews, Frederick C. *The Tragedy of Manners: Moral Drama in the Later Novels of Henry James.* 1957; rpt. Hamden, Conn.: Archon-Shoe String, 1971.

Dove, John Roland. "Tragic Consciousness in Isabel Archer." *Studies in American Literature.* Louisiana State University Studies, Humanities Series No. 8. Ed. Waldo McNeir and Leo B. Levy. Baton Rouge: Louisiana State University Press, 1960, pp. 78-94.

Dupee, F. W. *Henry James.* 1951; rpt. New York: William Morrow, 1974.

Dupee, F. W., ed. *The Question of Henry James: A Collection of Critical Essays.* London: Wingate, 1947.

Eakin, Paul John. *The New England Girl: Cultural Ideals in Hawthorne, Stowe, Howells, and James.* Athens, Ga.: University of Georgia Press, 1976.

Edel, Leon. *Henry James: The Untried Years 1843-1870, The Conquest of London 1870-1881, The Middle Years 1882-1895, The Treacherous Years 1895-1901, The Master 1901-1916.* 5 vols. Philadelphia: J. B. Lippincott, 1953-72.

Edel, Leon. Introduction to *The Portrait of a Lady.* By Henry James. Boston: Houghton Mifflin, 1963.

Edel, Leon, and Dan H. Laurence. *A Bibliography of Henry James.* 2nd ed. rev. London: Hart-Davis, 1961.

Eliot, T. S. "On Henry James: In Memory." In *The Question of Henry James: A Collection of Critical Essays.* Ed. F. W. Dupee. London: Wingate, 1947, pp. 123-33.

Felman, Shoshana. "Turning the Screw of Interpretation." *Yale French Studies,* 55/56 (1977), 94-207.

Freud, Sigmund. *The Complete Psychological Works of Sigmund Freud.* Trans. James Strachey. The Standard Edition. 24 vols. London: Hogarth Press, 1953-62.

Fryer, Judith. *The Faces of Eve: Women in the Nineteenth-Century American Novel.* New York: Oxford University Press, 1976.

Gass, William H. "The High Brutality of Good Intentions." *Accent,*
18 (Winter, 1958), 62-71. Rpt. in *Perspectives on James's The
Portrait of a Lady.* Ed. William T. Stafford. New York: New York
University Press, 1967, pp. 206-16.

Goode, John, ed. *The Air of Reality: New Essays on Henry James.*
London: Methuen, 1972.

Goode, John. "The Pervasive Mystery of Style: *The Wings of the
Dove.*" In *The Air of Reality: New Essays on Henry James.* Ed.
John Goode. London: Methuen, 1972, pp. 244-300.

Graham, Kenneth. *Henry James: The Drama of Fulfillment.*
London: Oxford University Press-Clarendon, 1975.

Holland, Laurence Bedwell. *The Expense of Vision: Essays on the
Craft of Henry James.* Princeton: Princeton University Press, 1964.

Horney, Karen. "Inhibited Femininity." In her *Feminine Psychology.*
Ed. Harold Kelman. New York: Norton, 1967, pp. 71-83.

Horney, Karen. *The Neurotic Personality of Our Time.* New York:
Norton, 1937.

Howells, William Dean. *Heroines of Fiction.* 2 vols. New York:
Harper, 1901.

Howells, William Dean. "Mr. Henry James's Later Work." In *The
Question of Henry James: A Collection of Critical Essays.* Ed. F.
W. Dupee. London: Wingate, 1947, pp. 26-39.

James, Alice. *The Diary of Alice James.* Ed. Leon Edel. London:
Rupert Hart-Davis, 1965.

James, Henry. *The American.* Ed. Matthew J. Bruccoli. Introd. Roy
Harvey Pearce. Boston: Houghton Mifflin, 1962.

James, Henry. *The American Scene.* Introd. Leon Edel. Bloomington: Indiana University Press, 1968.

James, Henry. *The Art of the Novel: Critical Prefaces by Henry
James.* Introd. R. P. Blackmur. New York: Scribners, 1962.

James, Henry. *Autobiography: A Small Boy and Others, Notes of a
Son and Brother, The Middle Years.* Ed. Frederick W. Dupee.
London: W. H. Allen, 1956.

James, Henry. *The Europeans: A Sketch.* Boston: Houghton Mifflin,
1878.

James, Henry. *French Poets and Novelists.* Introd. Leon Edel. New
York: Grosset and Dunlap, 1964.

James, Henry. *Henry James: Letters 1843-1875, Letters 1875-1883.* Ed.
Leon Edel. 2 vols. Cambridge, Mass.: Belknap-Harvard University
Press, 1974-75.

James, Henry. *The Letters of Henry James.* Ed. Percy Lubbock. 2
vols. New York: Scribners, 1920.

James, Henry. "The Manners of American Women: Part IV." *Harper's Bazar*, July 1907, pp. 646-51.

James, Henry. "The Modern Warning." In *The Complete Tales of Henry James*. Ed. Leon Edel. Vol. VII. Philadelphia and New York: Lippincott, 1963, pp. 15-86.

James, Henry. *The Notebooks of Henry James*. Ed. F. O. Matthiessen and Kenneth B. Murdock. New York: Oxford University Press, 1947.

James, Henry. *The Novels and Tales of Henry James*. The New York Edition. 24 vols. New York: Scribners, 1908-9.

James, Henry. *The Question of Our Speech; The Lesson of Balzac: Two Lectures*. Boston: Houghton Mifflin, 1905.

James, Henry. "The Speech of American Women: Part I." *Harper's Bazar*. November 1906, pp. 979-82.

Kristeva, Julia. "Oscillation Between Power and Denial." Trans. Marilyn A. August. In *New French Feminisms*. Ed. Elaine Marks and Isabelle De Courtivron. Amherst: The University of Massachusetts Press, 1980, pp. 165-67.

Krook, Dorothea. *The Ordeal of Consciousness in Henry James*. Cambridge: Cambridge University Press, 1962.

Krupnick, Mark L. *"The Golden Bowl:* Henry James's Novel About Nothing." *English Studies*, 57 (1976), 533-40.

Lacan, Jacques. *Ecrits: A Selection*. Trans. Alan Sheridan. London: Tavistock, 1977.

Lacan, Jacques. *The Four Fundamental Concepts of Psycho-Analysis*. Trans. Alan Sheridan. Ed. Jacques-Alain Miller. London: The Hogarth Press and The Institute of Psycho-Analysis, 1977.

Laing, R. D. *The Politics of the Family and Other Essays*. New York: Vintage-Random House, 1969.

Lebowitz, Naomi. *The Imagination of Loving: Henry James's Legacy to the Novel*. Detroit: Wayne State University Press, 1965.

Lewis, R. W. B. "The Vision of Grace: James's *The Wings of the Dove.*" *Modern Fiction Studies*, 3 (1957), 33-40.

Matthiessen, F. O. *Henry James: The Major Phase*. New York: Oxford University Press, 1944.

Matthiessen, F. O. *The James Family*. New York: Knopf, 1948.

McLean, Robert C. "'Love by the Doctor's Direction': Disease and Death in *The Wings of the Dove.*" *Papers on Language and Literature*, 8, supplement (1972), 128-48.

Mogen, David. "Agonies of Innocence: The Governess and Maggie Verver." *American Literary Realism*, 9 (1976), 231-42.

Mowbray, J. P. "The Apotheosis of Henry James." *Critic*, 41 (1902),

409-14. Rpt. in *Henry James: The Critical Heritage*. Ed. Roger Gard. New York: Barnes and Noble, 1968, pp. 326-31.

Mull, Donald L. *Henry James's "Sublime Economy": Money As Symbolic Center in the Fiction*. Middletown, Conn.: Wesleyan University Press, 1973.

Nettels, Elsa. "The Scapegoats and Martyrs of Henry James." *Colby Library Quarterly*, 10 (1974), 413-27.

Niemtzow, Annette. "Marriage and the New Woman in *The Portrait of a Lady*." *American Literature*, 47 (1975), 377-95.

Nowell-Smith, Simon. *The Legend of the Master*. London: Constable, 1947.

Nuhn, Ferner. *The Wind Blew from the East*. New York: Harper Brothers, 1940.

Patterson, Rebecca. "Two Portraits of a Lady." *Midwest Quarterly*, 1 (1960), 343-61.

Pearce, Roy Harvey. Introducton to *The American*. By Henry James. Ed. Matthew J. Bruccoli. Boston: Houghton Mifflin, 1962, pp. v-xxi.

Pearson, Gabriel. "The Novel to End All Novels: *The Golden Bowl*." In *The Air of Reality: New Essays on Henry James*. Ed. John Goode. London: Methuen, 1972, pp. 301-62.

Perloff, Marjorie. "Cinderella Becomes the Wicked Stepmother: *The Portrait of a Lady* as Ironic Fairy Tale." *Nineteenth-Century Fiction*, 23 (1969), 413-33.

Poirier, Richard. *The Comic Sense of Henry James: A Study of the Early Novels*. New York: Oxford University Press, 1967.

Rahv, Philip. "The Heiress of All the Ages." In his *Image and Idea: Twenty Essays on Literary Themes*. Rev. ed. Norfolk, Conn.: New Directions, 1957, pp. 51-76.

Riesman, David. *The Lonely Crowd: A Study of the Changing American Character*. New Haven: Yale University Press, 1950.

Roszak, Theodore. "The Hard and the Soft: The Force of Feminism in Modern Times." In *Masculine/Feminine: Readings in Sexual Mythology and the Liberation of Women*. Ed. Betty Roszak and Theodore Roszak. New York: Harper and Row, 1969, pp. 87-104.

Sabistan, Elizabeth. "The Prison of Womanhood." *Comparative Literature*, 25 (1973), 336-51.

Samuels, Charles Thomas. *The Ambiguity of Henry James*. Urbana: University of Illinois Press, 1971.

Sandeen, Ernest. "*The Wings of the Dove* and *The Portrait of a Lady*: A Study of Henry James's Later Phase." *PMLA*, 69 (1954), 1060-75. Rpt. in *Perspectives on James's The Portrait of a Lady*. Ed.

William T. Stafford. New York: New York University Press, 1967, pp. 187-205.

Schneider, Daniel. *The Crystal Cage: Adventures of the Imagination in the Fiction of Henry James*. Lawrence, Kansas: The Regents Press of Kansas, 1978.

Schriber, Mary S. "Isabel Archer and Victorian Manners." *Studies in the Novel*, 8 (1976), 441-57.

Schroder, Maurice Z. "The Novel As A Genre." In *The Theory of the Novel*. Ed. Philip Stevick. New York: The Free Press, 1967, pp. 13-29.

Sears, Sallie. *The Negative Imagination: Form and Perspective in the Novels of Henry James*. Ithaca, N. Y.: Cornell University Press, 1968.

Snow, Lotus. "The Disconcerting Poetry of Mary Temple: A Comparison of the Imagery of *The Portrait of a Lady* and *The Wings of the Dove*." *New England Quarterly*, 31 (1958), 312-39.

Spender, Stephen. *The Destructive Element: A Study of Modern Writers and Beliefs*. London: Jonathan Cape, 1935.

Springer, Mary Doyle. *A Rhetoric of Literary Character: Some Women of Henry James*. Chicago: The University of Chicago Press, 1978.

Stafford, William T., ed. *Perspectives on James's The Portrait of a Lady*. New York: New York University Press, 1967.

Stein, William Bysshe. *"The Portrait of a Lady: Vis Inertiae." Western Humanities Review*, 13 (1959), 177-90. Rpt. in *Perspectives on James's The Portrait of a Lady*. Ed. William T. Stafford. New York: New York University Press, 1967, pp. 166-83.

Stelzig, Eugene L. "Henry James and the 'Immensities of Perception': Actors and Victims in *The Portrait of a Lady* and *The Wings of the Dove*." *Southern Humanities Review*, 11 (1977), 253-65.

Stubbs, Patricia. *Women and Fiction: Feminism and the Novel, 1880-1920*. London: Methuen, 1979.

Van Ghent, Dorothy. *The English Novel: Form and Function*. 1953; rpt. New York: Harper and Row, 1961.

Veeder, William. *Henry James: The Lessons of the Master*. Chicago: University of Chicago Press, 1975.

Wagenknecht, Edward. *Eve and Henry James: Portraits of Women and Girls in His Fiction*. Norman: University of Oklahoma Press, 1978.

Ward, J. A. *The Imagination of Disaster: Evil in the Fiction of Henry James*. Lincoln: University of Nebraska Press, 1961.

Ward, J. A. *The Search for Form: Studies in the Structure of James's Fiction*. Chapel Hill: University of North Carolina Press, 1967.

Ward, Susan P. "Painting and Europe in *The American.*" *American Literature*, 46 (1975), 566-73.

Wasserstrom, William. *Heiress of All the Ages: Sex and Sentiment in the Genteel Tradition.* Minneapolis: University of Minnesota Press, 1959.

Wegelin, Christof. *The Image of Europe in Henry James.* Dallas: Southern Methodist University Press, 1958.

Weinstein, Philip M. *Henry James and the Requirements of the Imagination.* Cambridge, Mass.: Harvard University Press, 1971.

Wilden, Anthony. "Lacan and the Discourse of the Other." In *The Language of the Self: The Function of Language in Psychoanalysis.* By Jacques Lacan. Trans. Anthony Wilden. New York: Dell, 1968, pp. 159-311.

Wilson, James D. "The Gospel According to Christopher Newman." *Studies in American Fiction*, 3 (1975), 83-88.

Winner, Viola Hopkins. *Henry James and the Visual Arts.* Charlottesville: The University Press of Virginia, 1970.

Yeazell, Ruth Bernard. *Language and Knowledge in the Late Novels of Henry James.* Chicago: University of Chicago Press, 1976.

Index